MW00827828

Essential
Rome

AAA Publishing 1000 AAA Drive, Heathrow, Florida 32746

Rome: Regions and Best places to see

Original text by Jane Shaw
Updated by Tim Jepson

American editor: G.K. Sharman

Edited, designed and produced by AA Publishing
© Automobile Association Developments Limited 2008
Maps © Automobile Association Developments Limited 2008

978-1-59508-224-4

Published in the United States by AAA Publishing,
1000 AAA Drive, Heathrow, Florida 32746
Published in the United Kingdom by AA Publishing

Color separation: MRM Graphics Ltd
Printed and bound in Italy by Printer Trento S.r.l.

A03164
Maps in this title produced from map data © 2007 Navigation Technologies BV. All
rights reserved. Map updates courtesy of MAIRDUMONT, Ostfildern, Germany
Transport map © Communicarta Ltd, UK

About this book

Symbols are used to denote the following categories:

✚	map reference to maps on cover	🚍	nearest bus/tram route
✉	address or location	🚉	nearest overground train station
☎	telephone number	🛳	nearest ferry stop
🕐	opening times	✈	nearest airport
👋	admission charge	❓	other practical information
🍴	restaurant or café on premises	ℹ	tourist information office
	or nearby	►	indicates the page where you will
🚇	nearest metro station		find a fuller description

This book is divided into six sections.

The essence of Rome pages 6–19
Introduction; Features; Food and drink;
Short break

Planning pages 20–33
Before you go; Getting there; Getting
around; Being there

Best places to see pages 34–55
The unmissable highlights of any visit
to Rome

Best things to do pages 56–69
Top activities; Stunning views; Places to
take the children and more

Exploring pages 70–171
The best places to visit in Rome,
organized by area

Excursions pages 172–183
Places to visit out of town

Maps
All map references are to the maps on
the covers. For example, the Pantheon
has the reference ✚ 7F – indicating the
grid square in which it is to be found

Admission prices
Inexpensive: up to €4
Moderate: €4–€7
Expensive: over €7

Hotel prices
Prices are per room per night:
€ inexpensive (up to €125);
€€ moderate (€125–€225);
€€€ expensive to luxury (over €225)

Restaurant prices
Price for a three-course meal per person,
without drinks:
€ inexpensive (under €25);
€€ moderate (€25–€50);
€€€ expensive (over €50)

Contents

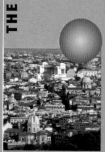

BEST THINGS TO DO

EXPLORING...

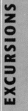

EXCURSIONS

The essence of...

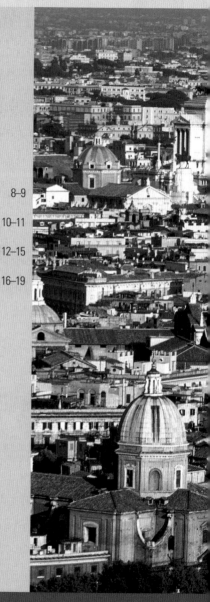

Central Rome on both sides of the Tiber (Tevere) is a city of contrasts. This busy modern capital is squeezed into a maze of old streets in which the layers of more than 2,000 years of history are superimposed on each other: ancient columns embedded in Renaissance palaces, baroque façades slapped onto the front of Romanesque churches and 1930s fascist office buildings nestling among it all. Not only is Rome the seat of the Italian government (both the President and the Prime Minister have their official residences here), but it is also an important place for the international film and fashion industries.

features

Rome has it all – a climate that gives sunny days at any time of year, a cuisine for all tastes and some of the best fine art and architecture in the world. This is a city of contrasts; a bustling, modern capital set amid ancient magnificence, where screeching *motorini* swoop past leisurely pedestrians, classical art competes for attention with high fashion, and a sunny day can suddenly throw up a sky-blackening storm with thunder-like cannon fire and rain that'll soak you in seconds.

It helps to approach Rome with a flexible attitude. You may not always be able to achieve what you set out to do (museums, shops, restaurants sometimes close suddenly for one reason or another), but don't worry. Even the streetlife, with its constantly changing parade of locals and visitors, is worth watching from a piazza café. There are intriguing juxtapositions everywhere: in narrow winding streets of terracotta buildings clothes boutiques nestle among family-run grocers, craft studios and art galleries.

The sunny weather helps create a relaxed way of life in which even the most simple transaction may

need far more time than you would have thought possible. On the other hand, is it really such a bad thing that lunch can take all afternoon? Once you adjust to the pace of life, you realize how much of Rome functions extremely efficiently, including the bus service, which gets you where you want in central Rome more or less when you want.

POPULATION

According to legend, Rome is roughly 2,700 years old. It has a population of about 2.5 million – up from 200,000 in 1870, when Italy became a unified nation (although there were well over 1 million people living in the city in the days of the empire). There are about 200,000 foreigner residents in Rome. About 10 million people arrive at Fiumicino airport every year. Over half the working population is in government administration; few work in industry (around 100,000), while some 600,000 people work in offices.

The city covers about 1,500sq km (585sq miles) and has 12 hills, having expanded from the original seven hills of Rome.

CLIMATE

The best months for visiting are April to June and September to October. The busiest time comes at Easter, when pilgrims swell the crowds of tourists.

In July and August temperatures can reach 40°C (104°F) and in August a lot of businesses close for the holidays. Early spring and late autumn are the wettest seasons (you can be unlucky at other times as well) – Rome has a similar annual rainfall to London but most falls over a few days. Even in winter the weather can be glorious, with maximum daily temperatures around 15°C (59°F) but, although it seldom snows, there can be bitingly cold winds in December, January and February.

food & drink

Italian cuisine is among the best (and, according to research, the most healthy) in the world. Each region has its own particular special dishes, making use of the abundant raw ingredients that grow there, and some typically Roman dishes also owe much to the history of the city and its occupants.

PASTA

Classic Roman pasta dishes are *spaghetti alla carbonara* with bacon, eggs and *pecorino* (matured sheep's milk cheese, often used as an alternative to parmesan); *pasta all'arrabbiata* (literally 'angry pasta') with tomatoes and fiery hot *peperoncino* (chilli); and *all'Amatriciana*, which is more or less the same with added bacon. *Pasta e ceci* is like a thick soup made with small pasta and chick peas, while *gnocchi* are hunger-busting potato dumplings served with butter and sage or tomato sauce.

MEAT AND OFFAL

Tradition has it that, while most of the butchered animal went to the rich, poor Romans had to make do with the offal. This has led to an abundance of dishes using tripe, liver, kidneys, heart, bone marrow (*ossobuco* is a bone out of which the marrow is scooped) and brains. Perhaps the most extreme of these is *pagliata*, which is the intestine of a milk-fed calf, often served with *bucatini*, the thin, tube-like pasta it resembles. The best place for eating offal is in Testaccio, where restaurants around the ex-abattoir Mattatoio have a long tradition of this type of cuisine.

Nowadays, however, even the most basic trattoria will offer its diners beef and veal steaks, sausages (often with brown lentils) and tasty lamb from nearby Abruzzo. *Saltimbocca alla Romana* ('jumps into the mouth') is veal wrapped in raw ham and cooked with sage.

FISH

Apart from the traditional *baccalà* (cod fillets fried in batter and served as a snack or first course in *pizzerie*), the range of fish in Rome is immense and includes seafood such as mussels, clams (especially in *spaghetti alle vongole*), squid and prawns.

VEGETABLES AND SNACK FOODS

Some of the vegetables common in Rome make good snacks – courgette (zucchini) flowers fried in batter, artichokes either steamed or baked, potato or spinach croquettes. *Supplì*, rice croquettes with melted mozzarella inside, are another between-meals filler. Other vegetables include *fave* (broad beans), often eaten with *pecorino* cheese in spring, spinach, broccoli, rocket (arugula) and *puntarelle*, a crispy salad vegetable served in a vinegary sauce with anchovies.

WINES AND DRINKS

In Rome most of the house white wines come from Frascati and the Castelli Romani that surround the city. Orvieto in Umbria is another source of inexpensive white wine.

House reds come from slightly farther afield than the whites, Montepulciano from Abruzzo (not to be confused with the Vino Nobile of Montepulciano in Tuscany, which is a top-quality wine) and Chianti from Tuscany.

As well as wine, Italy has a massive range of drinks to stimulate the appetite before you eat or to help you digest the meal afterwards. *Aperitivi* include Campari and Martini-type aromatics, *prosecco*, a light fizzy white wine and *analcolici*, non-alcoholic versions of Campari and Martini. *Digestivi* include grappas that range from firewater to the smoothest of the smooth and *amari*, those thick, sticky concoctions made with herbs.

DOLCI

If you don't opt for the ubiquitous *tiramisù*, for which every restaurant has its own subtly different recipe, you could finish your meal with a slice of cake (*torta*); chocolate, fruit or *torta della nonna* with custard and pine kernels. Especially in winter, you'll be offered *crème caramel*, *crème brûlée*, *panna cotta* ('cooked cream', a thick but light custard often served with berries) or ice-cream.

short break

If you only have a short time to visit Rome, or would like to get a complete picture of the city, here are the essentials:

● Go to the Vatican and marvel at Michelangelo's masterpieces in the Sistine Chapel (➤ 38–39).

● At St Peter's (➤ 36–37), look on the floor of the central aisle, where the lengths of other cathedrals' aisles are marked – see how your nearest cathedral back home measures up.

● Walk the streets at the Forum, where Julius Caesar trod (➤ 44–45).

● Do the Historic Centre walk (➤ 64–65) to take you past some of the most famous sights in the world.

● Try to imagine the Colosseum (➤ 42–43) full of raucous crowds, with wild animals and hapless humans fighting it out in the ring.

● Throw a coin into the Trevi Fountain (➤ 138), an act that is said to guarantee your return. Italian currency ends up in the coffers of the town council; foreign coins are donated to the Red Cross.

● Look down on Rome from on high (➤ 66–67 for suggested view points), and try to find the flattish dome with a hole in the middle, which is the Pantheon (➤ 50–51).

● Find a bar on Piazza Navona (➤ 52–53) or Campo de' Fiori (➤ 102), sip a drink and watch life saunter by.

● See Rome by night, preferably on foot. Many of the main monuments are floodlit and those that are not have an eerie beauty in the city's soft street lighting.

● Visit the church of Santa Maria in Cosmedin (➤ 89) to test your nerve with your hand in the *Bocca della Verità* (mouth of truth), which will bite if you tell a lie.

Planning

Before you go

WHEN TO GO

JAN	FEB	MAR	APR	MAY	JUN	JUL	AUG	SEP	OCT	NOV	DEC
7°C	8°C	11°C	14°C	18°C	23°C	26°C	25°C	22°C	18°C	13°C	9°C
45°F	46°F	52°F	57°F	64°F	73°F	79°F	77°F	72°F	64°F	55°F	48°F

🌥 High season 　🌤 Low season

Temperatures are the average daily maximum for each month, although temperatures of over 35°C (95°F) are likely in July and August. Average daily minimum temperatures are approximately 6 to 10°C (10–18°F) lower.

The best times to visit Rome are April to June and September to October, when the weather is generally fine but not too hot. Avoid July and August, when the city is not only stifling but also extremely crowded. August can also be humid and thundery. Winters are short but can be cold, notably in January and February, though these two months are also the quietest periods of the year. Snow is very rare. Heavy rain is possible in early spring and autumn.

The city is very busy around Easter and other major religious holidays, as well as during school holidays.

WHAT YOU NEED

		UK	Germany	USA	Netherlands	Spain
●	Required — Some countries require a passport to					
○	Suggested — remain valid for a minimum period (usually					
▲	Not required — at least six months) beyond the date of entry – check before you travel.					

	UK	Germany	USA	Netherlands	Spain
Passport (or National Identity Card where applicable)	●	●	●	●	●
Visa (regulations can change – check before you travel)	▲	▲	▲	▲	▲
Onward or Return Ticket	▲	▲	▲	▲	▲
Health Inoculations	▲	▲	▲	▲	▲
Health Documentation (► 23, Health Insurance)	●	●	▲	●	●
Travel Insurance	○	○	○	○	○
Driving Licence (national)	●	●	●	●	●
Car Insurance Certificate	○	○	○	○	○
Car Registration Document	●	●	●	●	●

WEBSITES

- Rome Tourist Authority
  www.romaturismo.it
- The Vatican
  www.vatican.va
- Museum information
  www.museionline.it

- Online museum and gallery
  booking www.ticketeria.it and
  www.pierreci.it
- Events and listings
  www.whatsoninrome.com

TOURIST OFFICES AT HOME

In the UK

Italian State Tourist Board
1 Princes Street
London W1R 2AY
☎ 020 7408 1254;
www.enit.it

In the USA

Italian State Tourist Board

630 Fifth Avenue, Suite 1565
New York NY 10111
☎ 212/245 4822;
www.italiantourism.com

Italian State Tourist Board
12400 Wilshire Boulevard
Suite 550, Los Angeles, CA 90025
☎ 310/820 0098

HEALTH INSURANCE

Nationals of EU and certain other countries receive reduced-cost emergency medical (including hospital) treatment and pay a percentage of prescribed medicines. You need a qualifying document (EHIC – European Health Insurance Card). Private medical insurance is still advised and is essential for all other visitors. Nationals of EU and certain other countries can obtain dental treatment at a reduced cost at dentists within the Italian health service. A qualifying document (EHIC) is needed.

TIME DIFFERENCES

GMT	Rome	Germany	USA (NY)	Netherlands	Spain
12 noon	1PM	1PM	7AM	1PM	1PM

Italy is one hour ahead of Greenwich Mean Time (GMT+1), but Italian Summer Time (GMT+2) operates from late March to late September.

NATIONAL HOLIDAYS

1 Jan *New Year's Day*
6 Jan *Epiphany*
Mar/Apr *Easter Monday*
25 Apr *Liberation Day*
1 May *Labour Day*
15 Aug *Assumption of the Virgin*

1 Nov *All Saints' Day*
8 Dec *Immaculate Conception*
25 Dec *Christmas Day*
26 Dec *St Stephen's Day*

Banks, businesses and most shops and museums close on these days. Rome celebrates its patron saint (St Peter) on 29 June, but generally most places remain open.

WHAT'S ON WHEN

January

New Year's Day: public holiday.
6 Jan: Epiphany, public holiday. Traditionally the *befana* (witch) leaves presents for children.

February

Week leading up to Shrove Tuesday: *Carnevale*, streets full of adults and children in fancy dress.
Shrove Tuesday: *Martedi grasso* celebrations (in costume) in Piazza Navona (➤ 52–53) and elsewhere.

March/April

9 Mar: cars, buses and taxis blessed at the church of San Francesca Romana (the patron saint of motorists) in the Forum (➤ 44–45).
Mid-Mar onwards: Spanish Steps (➤ 146–147) decorated with huge azalea plants.
Good Friday: Pope leads the ceremony of the Stations of the Cross at the Colosseo (Colosseum) (➤ 42–43).
Easter Sunday: papal address at St Peter's.
Easter Monday: public holiday.
21 Apr: Rome's birthday, bands and orchestras perform at Campidoglio, (➤ 46–47), Piazza di Spagna (➤ 146) and elsewhere.
25 Apr: Liberation Day, public holiday to commemorate the Allies' liberation of Rome from the Nazis in 1944.

May

1 May: Labour Day, public holiday, no public transportation, huge free rock concert in Piazza di San Giovanni in Laterano.
Early May: horse show at Piazza di Siena.
Mid-May to Oct: rose garden above Circo Massimo (► 78) open to the public.
Mid-May: International tennis tournament held in Rome.

June/July

Mid-Jun to Sep: outdoor concerts, cinemas, fairs and other arts events all over the city.
End Jun to mid-Sep: *Estate Romana*. The ever-expanding festival offering open-air cinema, music, drama and arts events around the city.
Mid- to late Jul: *Festa de Noantri*, stalls, concerts and other cultural events in Trastevere.

August

15 Aug: *Ferragosto*, public holiday, lots of shops, restaurants, bars and businesses close for a week or more.

October

Early Oct: wine festivals in towns near Rome, and a small one in Trastevere.

November

1 Nov: All Saints' Day, public holiday.
Mid-Nov: the new season's *vini novelli* ready for drinking.

December

Beginning Dec to 6 Jan: Christmas fair in Piazza Navona (► 52–53).
8 Dec: Immaculate Conception, public holiday.
Christmas time: *presepi* (nativity scenes) on display in churches and main piazzas.
25 Dec: Christmas Day, public holiday, papal address in St Peter's Square.
31 Dec: New Year's Eve celebrations, fireworks and concerts in Piazza del Popolo (► 145) and elsewhere in the city.

Getting there

BY AIR

Leonardo da Vinci (Fiumicino) Airport

36km (22 miles) to central Rome

🚈 30 or 45 minutes

🚌 50 minutes

🚗 40 minutes

Ciampino Airport

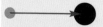

15km (9 miles) to central Rome

🚈 20 minutes, plus 15-min bus to train

🚌 30 minutes

🚗 30 minutes

Rome has two main airports: Leonardo da Vinci (better known as Fiumicino) and Ciampino. The website for both airports is www.adr.it. Most UK and other European and international carriers fly to Fiumicino. Low-cost and charter airlines usually fly to Ciampino. There are many non-stop flights to Rome from London (Heathrow, Gatwick and Stansted) as well as Birmingham and Manchester in the UK, most major European cities and many US and Canadian cities. Flights from Melbourne and Sydney make one stop, usually in Bangkok; from other cities in Australia and New Zealand, the best connections are in Hong Kong or Singapore.

The Terravision airport–city bus shuttle service operates between both airports and Stazione Termini (www.terravision.it, €8 single from Ciampino, €7 from Fiumicino).

Air fares tend to be highest at Easter, Christmas and during the summer. Best prices are obtained the further you reserve in advance, but check airlines, travel agents, newspapers and the internet for special offers. Non-direct flights via hub airports such as Heathrow may offer substantial savings.

BY RAIL

Most international and national rail services arrive at Rome's main railway station, officially known as Stazione Centrale Giovanni Paolo II, but almost universally known as Termini. A few long-distance, sleeper and international train services may stop at Stazione Roma Tiburtina, a much less convenient suburban station with train and bus links to Termini and other parts of the city. For further rail information, look up the Italian Railways website, www.trenitalia.it

Train fares are usually the same price or more expensive than air fares for equivalent journeys. Numerous fast and overnight services operate to Rome from most European capitals, with connections from major towns.

BY CAR

The main A1 autostrada (toll motorway) links Rome with Florence and the north. The A2 links the city with Naples and points to the south. The A24 runs east to the Abruzzo mountains and Adriatic coast. The motorways and most other main roads into the city connect with the Grand Raccordo Anulare (GRA), the Rome ring road. This can be very busy at peak times, with frequent delays. The difficulty of parking and heavy traffic mean it is not advisable to drive into the city, but if you must, ask your hotel for the best GRA exit and approach.

BY BUS

Eurolines (0870 514 3219 in the UK, 055 357 110 in Italy; www.eurolines.com) provides long-distance buses to Rome from the UK and elsewhere in Europe, but the services are much slower and often no cheaper than flights or train services. Most long-distance buses run to Piazza dei Cinquecento, near Stazione Termini .

BY SEA

Ferries and cruise ships run to ports north and south of Rome from Sardinia, southern France, Sicily and elsewhere, generally to Civitavecchia, about an hour's drive north of the city.

Getting around

PUBLIC TRANSPORT

Internal flights Services throughout the country are provided by Alitalia – the national airline (☎ 06 65641; www.alitalia.it). The flight time to Rome from Milan is 65 minutes; from Florence 75 minutes; and from Naples 45 minutes. Departures are *Partenze Nazionali*, arrivals *Arrivi Nazionali*.

Trains Italian State Railways (Ferrovie dello Stato, or FS) provides an efficient service. Almost all long-distance trains to Rome arrive and depart from Stazione Termini (some fast trains use Stazione Roma Tiburtina, ► 27). Stazione Termini is shut from midnight to 5am, during which time trains stop at other city stations. For timetable information, see www.trenitalia.it.

Long-distance buses There is no national bus company, but COTRAL (☎ 800 150008, Mon–Sat) has the major presence in Rome, serving the Lazio region. Buses depart from numerous points throughout the city. For details ask at the nearest tourist information office.

Urban transport Buses (orange, red-grey or green), plus trams in the outer districts, are the best way to get around Rome, although the complexity of the routes can be daunting. Bus or tram stops *(fermata)* have yellow signs. You must have a ticket before boarding at the rear *(salita)* and you must stamp your ticket in the machine on board. Exit through the middle door *(uscita)*.

The underground/subway *(Metropolitana or Metrò)* has only two lines: *Linea A* (red) runs from Battistini to Anagnina in the southeast. *Linea B* (blue) runs from Rebibbia in the northeast to Laurentina in the southwest. Buy tickets from machines at the metro stations. Station entrances are marked by a white 'M' on a red background.

FARES AND TICKETS

Holders of an International Student Identity Card (ISIC) or an International Youth Card (IYC) can take advantage of discounts on transportation. Citizens of the EU and some other countries, who are over the age of 60, may receive discounts on public transport by showing their passport.

TAXIS

You can hail a taxi on the street, find one at a taxi rank (at stations and major *piazze*) or phone 06 3570, 88177, 4994 or 5551). There is an initial charge and a rate for each kilometre. Traffic can mean stiff meter increases and there are Sunday and late-night supplements.

DRIVING

- Drive on the right.
- Seat belts must be worn in front seats at all times and in rear seats where fitted.
- Random breath-testing takes place. Never drive under the influence of alcohol.
- Fuel *(benzina)* is more expensive in Italy than in Britain and most other European countries. All except small garages in out-of-the-way places sell unleaded fuel *(senza piombo)*. Outside urban areas, filling stations are open 7am to 12:30pm and 3 to 7:30pm. Motorway service stations are open 24 hours. Credit cards are not widely accepted.
- Speed limits on motorways *(autostrade)*, which have tolls: 130kph/80mph.
- If you break down, ring 116, giving your registration number and type of car and the nearest ACI (Automobile Club d'Italia) office will be informed to assist you. You will be towed to the nearest ACI garage. This service is free to foreign-registered vehicles or cars rented from Rome or Milan airports (you will need to produce your passport).

CAR RENTAL

Car rental *(autonoleggio)* can be found at airports, the main rail station and city offices, but driving in Rome is not recommended and not cheap.

Being there

TOURIST OFFICES
Visitor Centres
Via Parigi 5 and 11
☎ 06 3660 4399/06 488991
🕐 Mon–Sat 8–7

Leonardo da Vinci (Fiumicino) Airport
☎ 06 3600 4399
🕐 Mon–Sun 8–7

Stazione Termini (main rail station)
☎ 06 4890 6300 🕐 8am–9pm

Info-Tourism Kiosks
Largo Carlo Goldoni, Via del Corso
☎ 06 6813 6061 🕐 9–6

Palazzo delle Esposizioni,
Via Nazionale
☎ 06 4782 4525 🕐 9–6

Fori Imperiali,
Piazza del Tempio della Pace
☎ 06 6992 4307 🕐 9–6

Fontana di Trevi, Via Marco
Minghetti
☎ 06 678 2988 🕐 9–6

Santa Maria Maggiore, Via
dell'Olmata
☎ 06 474 0995 🕐 9–6

Trastevere, Piazza Sidney Sonnio
☎ 06 5833 3457 🕐 9–6

MONEY
The euro (€) is the official currency of Italy. Money can be exchanged at airports, exchange kiosks and in banks. Cash withdrawals can also be made from ATM machines with credit and debit cards.

TIPS/GRATUITIES

Yes ✓ No ✗		
Hotels (if service included)	✓	10–15%
Restaurants (if service not included)	✓	10–15%
Cafés/bars (if service not included)	✓	€1 min
Taxis	✓	15%
Porters	✓	€1
Chambermaids	✓	€1 per day
Toilet attendants	✓	10 cents min

POSTAL AND INTERNET SERVICES

The city's main post office is on Piazza San Silvestro 19.
🕐 Mon–Fri 9–6:30 or 7:30, Sat 8:30–1. Closed Sun ☎ 06 6771;
www.poste.it
Vatican City has a separate postal system, with a post office in
St Peter's Square.
🕐 8:30–6 or 6:30 (6 Sat). Closed Sun ☎ 06 6988 3406

TELEPHONES

Almost every bar has a telephone and there are also many in public
places. Buy phonecards from Telecom Italia (TI) offices, tobacconists,
stations and other public places. Coin operated telephones are now rare.

International dialling codes

UK: 00 44
Germany: 00 49
USA: 00 1

Netherlands: 00 31
Spain: 00 34

Calling Italy from abroad

From the UK dial 00 39
From the US dial 011 39

Emergency telephone numbers

Police: 113
Carabinieri: 112
Fire: 115

Any emergency (including
ambulance): 118
Road assistance (ACI): 116

EMBASSIES AND CONSULATES

UK ☎ 06 4220 0001;
www.britain.it
Germany ☎ 06 492131
USA ☎ 06 46741;

www.usembassy.it
Netherlands ☎ 06 367 671
Spain ☎ 06 684 0401

HEALTH ADVICE

Sun advice Rome can get oppressively hot in
summer, particularly in July and August. Cover
up with loose clothing, apply sunscreen, seek
out the shade and drink plenty of fluids.
Pharmacies A pharmacy *(farmacia)*, recognized
by a green cross sign, will have highly trained

staff able to offer medical advice on minor ailments and provide prescribed and non-prescribed medicines and drugs.

Safe water Rome is famed for its drinking water, which is generally safe, even from outdoor fountains (unless you see a sign saying *acqua non potabile*). However, most Romans prefer to drink bottled mineral water.

PERSONAL SAFETY

Petty theft poses the biggest threat. The police *(polizia)* to whom thefts should be reported wear light-blue trousers and dark-blue jackets.

- Take care of your belongings on the 64 bus to St Peter's and around the Termini train station.
- Carry shoulder bags not on your shoulder but slung across your body.
- Scooter-borne bag-snatchers can be foiled if you keep away from the edge of the road.
- Do not put anything down on a café or restaurant table.
- Lock car doors and never keep valuables in your car.

ELECTRICITY

The power supply is 220 volts (125 volts in parts of Rome). Round two- or three-hole sockets take plugs of two round pins, or sometimes three pins in a vertical row. British visitors should bring an adaptor; US visitors a voltage transformer.

OPENING HOURS

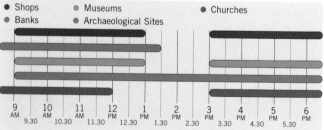

Shops and museums are opening for increasingly longer hours. Some museums, supermarkets and shops in tourist areas may not close at lunchtime. Most shops close Sunday. Some banks open until 3 or 4pm. Many museums close around 1pm on Sunday and do not open Mondays.

LANGUAGE

Many Romans speak English but you will be better received if you at least attempt to communicate in Italian. Italian words are pronounced phonetically. Every vowel and consonant (except 'h') is sounded. The accent usually (but not always) falls on the penultimate syllable.

yes	*sì*	help!	*aiuto!*
no	*no*	today	*oggi*
please	*per favore*	tomorrow	*domani*
thank you	*grazie*	yesterday	*ieri*
hello	*ciao*	how much?	*quanto?*
goodbye	*arrivederci*	open	*aperto*
excuse me	*mi scusi*	closed	*chiuso*
hotel	*albergo*	...one/two people	*...per una/due*
room	*camera*		*persona/e*
...single/double	*...singola/doppia*	reservation	*prenotazione*
...one/two nights	*...per una/due*	rate	*tariffa*
	notte/i	breakfast	*prima colazione*
bank	*banco*	foreign exchange	*cambio con l'estero*
exchange office	*cambio*	foreign currency	*valuta estera*
post office	*posta*	pound sterling	*sterlina*
cashier	*cassiere/a*	American dollar	*dollaro*
credit card	*carta di credito*	bank note	*banconota*
restaurant	*ristorante*	water	*acqua*
café	*caffè*	starter	*il primo*
menu	*menù/carta*	main course	*il secondo*
wine list	*lista dei vini*	dessert	*dolci*
drink	*bevanda*	the bill	*il conto*
aeroplane	*aeroplano*	bus	*autobus*
airport	*aeroporto*	bus station	*autostazione*
train	*treno*	ticket	*biglietto*
train station	*stazione ferroviaria*	...single/return	*...andata sola/*
timetable	*orario*		*andata e ritorno*

Best places to see

1 Basilica di San Pietro

www.vatican.va

Whether you find its opulence impressive or over the top, the sheer size of the world's most important church will not leave you unmoved.

Emperor Constantine built a shrine to St Peter over his tomb and near where he had been crucified in the Circus of Nero. As the fortunes of Rome and

the newly established Christian religion rose and fell, the building saw periods of embellishment fluctuating with sackings and destruction, and had been much altered by the time Pope Nicholas V ordered its restoration in the mid-15th century. Work did not get under way until about 50 years later, when Pope Julius II appointed Bramante as the architect for a new basilica in 1503. Another 123 years, and interventions from many of the most important architects and artists of the time were to pass before the new basilica was consecrated. The basic floor plan is as Bramante designed it, 187m (613ft) long; Michelangelo designed the 132.5m (435ft) high dome, Carlo Maderno the façade and Bernini the oval colonnade that surrounds the piazza in front of the basilica.

Inside, on the right, is Michelangelo's *Pietà* of 1499. Other gems include a 13th-century bronze statue of St Peter, whose foot has been worn away by the touch of pilgrims; Bernini's massive 20m (66ft) high *baldacchino*, or altar canopy (under which only the Pope can celebrate Mass), his monuments to popes Urban VIII and Alexander VII and the tabernacle in the shape of a temple.

✚ 2E ✉ Piazza San Pietro ☎ 06 6988 1662 ⊗ Mid-Mar to end Sep daily 7–7; Oct to mid-Mar 7–6 ✋ Free to Basilica; access to roof moderate ⊜ Ottaviano 🚌 64 to Piazza San Pietro; 23, 32, 49, 81, 492, 990 to Piazza del Risorgimento ❓ Tours of the necropolis in English must be booked through the Uffizio degli Scavi in St Peter's Square

2 Cappella Sistina and the Musei Vaticani

www.vatican.va

Michelangelo's masterpiece is one of today's wonders of the world, fittingly reached via the rooms of one of the world's greatest art collections.

It is impossible to do justice to the Vatican Museums in one visit, but you can take in the main attractions by selecting one of several routes suggested on leaflets available at the entrance, or by concentrating on highlights, such as the Museo Pio-Clementino (▶ 165); the frescoes in the Stanze

di Rafaello (Raphael Rooms, ➤ 168); and, of course, the Capella Sistina (Sistine Chapel).

Michelangelo painted the Sistine Chapel ceiling between 1508 and 1512, crouching for hours on the scaffolding as Pope Julius II chivvied him on from below. A thorough cleaning in the 1980s and 1990s, during which some of the garments that more puritanical popes had had painted onto Michelangelo's scantily clad biblical figures were stripped off, restored the original vibrant hues. The ceiling tells the story of the Creation, in which a pink-clad God nips around dividing light from darkness and water from land before going on to create the sun, the moon, Adam and Eve. The last four panels show the birth of original sin and the story of Noah. On the chapel's end wall is Michelangelo's much later *Last Judgement*. By the time he started this in 1534 he was racked with ill-health and thoughts of his own mortality, and it took him until 1541 to complete. The flayed skin held up by St Bartholomew (to Christ's left) is believed to be a self-portrait. The other walls of the chapel were painted with episodes from the lives of Christ and Moses by, among others, Botticelli and Perugino.

✚ 2D–E ✉ Viale Vaticano 🕐 Mar–end Oct Mon–Fri 10–4:45, Sat 10–1:45; Nov–end Feb Mon–Sat 10–1:45. Last Sun of each month 10–1:45 ✋ Expensive; free last Sun of month 🍴 Choice of restaurants and bars (€) 🚇 Ottaviano 🚌 23, 32, 49, 81, 492, 990 to Piazza del Risorgimento ❓ Guided tours available ☎ 06 6988 5100. It is quieter to visit in the afternoon and best to avoid Saturdays ℹ Vatican Tourist Office ☎ 06 6988 4947

3 Castel Sant'Angelo

This powerful monument on the Tiber symbolizes almost 2,000 years of Roman history, from Hadrian to Italian Unification.

Castel Sant'Angelo was central to the history of the papacy and the defence of the city until 1886, when it was turned into a museum. It is a labyrinth of a place, both literally and historically.

Emperor Hadrian (AD117–138) built Castel Sant'Angelo as a mausoleum to himself. Visitors today enter via the original Roman passageway, up which the funeral procession passed. This joins one of the medieval ramps that were added when the tomb was converted into a defensive fortress. The dark ramp finally opens onto a courtyard (originally the funerary garden), where now there is Montelupo's statue (1544) of an angel sheathing a sword, commemorating (along with the monument's name) a legendary event in which an angel was seen over Rome at the end of a plague in AD590.

Off the courtyard (with its Michelangelo façade from 1514) is the *Sala di Apollo* (1548), exquisitely decorated with ornate *grotteschi* (frescoes); illuminated windows in the floor give you

a view down to the underground corridors that led to a notorious papal prison. Following Medici Pope Clement VII's seven-month siege inside the Castello (1527), the popes felt they needed more sumptuous apartments. Farnese Pope Paul III (1534–49) commissioned the magnificent *Sala Paolina*, with its beautiful frescoes and *trompe l'oeil* doors. Off the library (with gorgeous stucco work) is the wood-lined papal treasury, the room believed to have held Hadrian's tomb, although the whereabouts of his remains are a mystery. The tour finishes with a walk around the ramparts.

✚ 5E ✉ Lungotevere Castello 50 ☎ 06 681 9111/ 06 3996 7600 (recorded information) 🕐 Tue–Sun 9–7:30; ticket office closes at 6:30 ✋ Moderate 🍴 Café (€) Ⓜ Lepanto 🚌 34, 40, 62 to Piazza Cavour

4 Colosseo

Built in the first century AD as a gift to the Romans, this dignified, round monument is the city's most recognizable symbol.

Emperor Vespasian commissioned the Colosseum to fill the site of a huge lake that his predecessor, Nero, had had excavated for his own private use. The massive circus, with a capacity of more than 55,000, was used for popular, bloodthirsty spectator sports. In spite of centuries of use as an unofficial marble quarry for Renaissance and baroque builders, much of the outer shell has survived, showing the four arched tiers (each arch held a statue) behind which staircases and galleries led to the auditorium. Seating was segregated according to gender and status; the emperor's box was at the southern end (opposite today's main entrance) and below him sat the Vestal Virgins.

Nearly all the events staged here guaranteed the bloody death of human participants. Gladiators were usually slaves, prisoners of war or condemned prisoners, but the enthusiastic following that a successful gladiator provoked encouraged some upper-class men to train for combat. Other spectacles involved mismatched rivals fighting to the death with nets, tridents and other weapons; fights against wild animals were also popular. The labyrinth of underground

passages, lifts and cages through which these unfortunate beasts were channelled into the ring can be seen under the arena. Gladiatorial combat was banned in the fifth century, and changing public tastes led to the Colosseum falling out of use by the sixth century.

✠ 19J ✉ Piazza del Colosseo ☎ 06 3996 7700; reserve online at www.pierreci.it ⏰ May–end Sep daily 9–7:30; Apr, Oct daily 9–6:30; Nov–end Mar daily 9–4:30; last ticket 1 hour before closing ✋ Expensive; joint ticket with Palatino Ⓜ Colosseo 🚌 60, 75, 85, 87, 117, 175 to Piazza del Colosseo ❓ English-language tours several times a day

5 Foro Romano

This was the social, economic and political core of ancient Rome, where people came to shop, consult lawyers or gossip.

Before entering the Foro, or Forum, look down on it from behind the Campidoglio (➤ 46). To your left is the Arch of Septimius Severus, erected in AD203 to celebrate his victory over the Parthians; behind it, to the right, is the Column of Phocas, AD608, erected to thank the Byzantine Emperor, Phocas, for giving the Pantheon (➤ 50–51) to the pope.

Left of the main public entrance to the Forum is the Basilica Aemilia, a place for business; look for traces of the coins that were fused into the floor when the Basilica was burned down in the fifth century. Next to the Basilica, along the Via Sacra (Sacred Way), is the third-century Curia (rebuilt in the 1930s), where the Senate met; the slightly curved platform outside it is the rostrum on which political speeches and orations were made. Opposite the Curia is the first-century BC Basilica Julia and to its left is the Temple of Castor and

Pollux, with its three beautiful remaining columns. The round building is the Temple of Vesta, where a fire was kept burning continually by the 16 Vestal Virgins who lived in the elegant villa behind it. On the other side of the Forum are the three massive vaults of the fourth-century Basilica of Maxentius and Constantine, much studied by Renaissance artists and architects. To its left is the fourth-century Temple of Romulus, under which you can see some dank little rooms, thought to be the remains of a much earlier brothel. The Arch of Titus is near the public exit; it was erected in the first century AD to celebrate the Emperor's sack of Jerusalem.

✚ 18H ✉ Via dei Fori Imperiali ☎ 06 3996 7700 🕐 9 to 1 hour before sunset 💷 Free 🚇 Colosseo 🚌 75, 85, 117, 175, 810, 850 to Via dei Fori Imperiali ❓ Guided tours are available in English

6 Musei Capitolini

www.museicapitolini.org

The Capitoline Museums are home to one of Europe's most impressive collections of ancient sculpture – started by the popes in the 15th century.

Michelangelo designed Rome's magnificent civic centre, although later architects finished the job. Today, only the salmon-pink Palazzo Senatorio is used for political purposes (the mayor's office), while the flanking buildings form the Campidoglio (or Capitoline) Museums.

On entering the restored Palazzo Nuovo, on the left, you are greeted by the enormous second-century bronze equestrian statue of Emperor Marcus Aurelius, which stood in the heart of the square until 1981. On the first floor in Room 1 (Sala 1) is

a superb, sensual *Dying Gaul;* like many sculptures here, this is a Roman copy in marble of an earlier Greek work. Roman heads abound, including portraits of philosophers (a whole roomful) and eminent citizens with elaborate hair. The erotic *Capitoline Venus* has a chamber to herself.

The Palazzo Nuovo links by underground passage – known as Gallery Junction – to the restored Palazzo dei Conservatori. In the Conservatori courtyard are giant hands, a head and feet – fragments from a colossal statue of Constantine found in the Forum. Upstairs, highlights include the creamy marble *Venus Esquilina* and the delightfully realistic first-century BC bronze *Spinario*, a young boy extracting a thorn from his foot. The *She Wolf Suckling Romulus and Remus,* in the Sala della Lupa, will be familiar to many – the symbol of Rome is reproduced everywhere. The wolf is thought to be an Etruscan bronze of the late sixth to early fifth centuries BC, to which the twins were added in the 16th century.

Paintings include works by Pietro da Cortona, Guido Reni, Tintoretto, Rubens, Van Dyck, Velázquez and Titan; Caravaggio's sensual *St John the Baptist* and Guercino's *Burial of St Petronilla* stand out.

✚ 17H ✉ Piazza del Campidoglio 1 ☎ 06 6710 2475/06 3996 7800 (recorded information) 🕐 Tue–Sun 9–8
✋ Expensive 🚌 44, 46, 75, 84, 715, 716 to Piazza Venezia

7 Palazzo Barberini

**A treasure trove of paintings from the
13th to the 16th centuries is housed in one
of Rome's grandest baroque palaces.**

Carlo Maderno's original design, begun in 1624 for
Barberini Pope Urban VIII, was embellished by
Bernini and Maderno's nephew Borromini. The latter
added the elegant oval staircase and the windows
of the upper floor which, using ingenious artificial
perspective, preserve the symmetry of the façade

while staying in proportion with the size of the actual rooms.

The palace was sold to the Italian state in 1949 and houses, together with Palazzo Corsini (➤ 112), the national collection of art – Galleria Nazionale d'Arte Antica. Extensive renovations are bringing the main rooms back to their original glory, the most spectacular of which is the *Gran Salone*, with its elaborate ceiling fresco, *Triumph of Divine Providence*, by Pietro da Cortona. Another highlight is the bedroom of Princess Cornelia Costanza Barberini and Prince Giulio Cesare Colonna di Sciarra.

Magnificent *quattrocento* panel paintings include an ethereal *Annunciation* by Filippo Lippi and a *Madonna and Saints* by Alunno. The highlights of the collection are the 16th- and 17th-century paintings: Andrea del Sarto's magical *Sacra Famiglia*; Raphael's *La Fornarina* (widely believed to be a portrait of the baker's daughter, who was his mistress, although some maintain it is in fact a picture of a courtesan and was painted by Giulio Romano); a portrait of Urban VIII by Bernini (his genius lay more in sculpture and architecture); and works by El Greco, Bronzino, Guido Reni, Guercino and Caravaggio.

✚ 10E ✉ Via Quattro Fontane 13 ☎ 06 32810 (to reserve tickets); gallery 06 482 4184; reserve online at www.ticketeria.it 🕐 Tue–Sun 9–7 💰 Moderate
🚇 Barberini 🚌 52, 53, 56, 61, 62, 63, 80, 95, 116, 119 to Via del Tritone

8 Pantheon

Its massive circular interior, lit only by a round opening in the roof, is one of the most awe-inspiring sights of Rome.

Do not be misled by the inscription, *Agrippa fecit*, over its portals. Agrippa built an earlier version of this temple to all the gods but what we see today was erected by Emperor Hadrian in the early second century AD and, in spite of losing many of its opulent trimmings over the centuries, it remains much as he would have remembered it.

The dome is a semi-sphere 43.5m (144ft) in diameter, with walls 6m (18ft) thick. It was constructed by pouring concrete over a wooden framework. Originally the roof was covered with bronze cladding, which was stripped by Constantine II in the seventh century to decorate Constantinople. One thousand years later, Bernini took the remaining bronze from the roof beams

to build the canopy (*baldacchino*) in St Peter's (► 36–37). The building's huge bronze doors, however, have survived since Roman times. The marble floor is a 19th-century reconstruction of the original design and the interior has been cleaned and touched up to restore its subtly vibrant shades.

It was one of the first Roman temples to be converted into a church (by Pope Boniface IV when Emperor Phocas donated the building to him; consecrated AD609) and over the centuries several leading Italians, including the painter Raphael, have been buried here.

✚ 7F ✉ Piazza della Rotonda ☎ 06 6830 0230 🕔 Mon–Sat 8:30–7:30, Sun 9–6; public hols 9–1 🎫 Free 🚌 116 to Piazza della Rotonda; 30, 40, 46, 62, 63, 64, 70, 81 and all other services to Largo di Torre Argentina ❓ Sometimes used for concerts and special services

Piazza Navona

One of the world's most beautiful squares owes its elongated shape to the ancient Roman stadium over which it was built.

Although the best effect can be had by approaching Piazza Navona from the southeast, no matter which of the narrow streets you take, this massive space in Rome's cramped historical heart is always breathtaking. To its north are remains of the entrance to the stadium that Emperor Domitian built in the first century AD.

The piazza's focal point is Bernini's spectacular Fontana dei Fiumi (Fountain of the Rivers, 1651), featuring symbolic representations of the Ganges, Danube, Plate and Nile (blindfolded because its source was then unknown), clinging to a massive artificial cliff-face while sea monsters lurk beneath. The figure at the middle of the fountain to the southeast is another Bernini work, *Il Moro* (the moor); the figures of Neptune and others on the third fountain are 19th-century.

This has always been a hub of Roman social life; there was a market here for centuries and the piazza used to be flooded in August to form a vast watery playground for rich and poor alike. Today it is flooded by musicians, artists, locals and visitors who flock to its bars for hours at a time.

✚ 6F ✉ Piazza Navona 🍴 Lots of bars, tend to be expensive, but worth it 🚌 40, 46, 62, 64 to Corso Vittorio Emanuele II; 30, 70, 81, 87, 116, 492, 628 to Corso del Rinascimento ❓ December Christmas fair (➤ 25)

10 San Clemente

A 12th-century church, on top of a 4th-century one, on top of an ancient shrine of Mithras – visit San Clemente for a walk through Rome's multi-layered history.

Even without its hidden depths, San Clemente is one of the prettiest churches in Rome, with its 12th-century apse mosaic, *The Triumph of the Cross*, showing details of animals, birds and humans in flower-filled fields and its simple, sixth-century choir stall, originally in the earlier church building. The spiralling column next to the choir stall is a 12th-century cosmati (➤ 89) mosaic candlestick. To the left of the entrance is the chapel of St Catherine, with 15th-century frescoes by

Masolini of her life and martyrdom on the original Catherine wheel.

However, the church's main claim to fame lies underneath, where the first layer contains the remains of a fourth-century church in which some fragments of ancient masonry and 11th-century frescoes, illustrating the life and miracles of St Clemente (martyred by being tied to an anchor and drowned) have been preserved among the foundations of the later church. There is also a large circular well that was probably used as a font.

Descending yet farther you come to the ancient Roman level, where the highlight is a cramped room with a small altar on which there is a relief of Mithras slaying a bull. The Mithraic cult arrived in Rome from Persia about the same time as Christianity and had a strong following, especially among soldiers (women were not allowed to join).

The route out takes you through the walls of several ancient Roman apartment blocks. Even lower, although not open to the public, are some fifth- or sixth-century catacombs.

✚ 20J ✉ Via di San Giovanni in Laterano ☎ 06 7045 1018 🕐 Mon–Sat 9–12:30, 3–6, Sun and public hols from 10 ✋ Moderate; free to upper church 🚇 Colosseo 🚌 85, 117, 850 to Via di San Giovanni in Laterano; 85, 87, 117, 175 to Piazza del Colosseo

Best things to do

Top activities

Explore: set off on two feet and take in Rome (▶ 4, 90, 110 for walk suggestions).

Eat: enjoy some traditional Roman cuisine at one of the restaurants in the heart of the city (▶ 129–132).

Head for the sky: climb to the top of the dome at St Peter's (▶ 36–37) for wonderful views across the city.

Lunch: spend all afternoon having lunch (▶ 96–98, 129–132, 154–155, 170 for ideas).

Be blessed: attend the Pope's blessing. The Pope addresses the crowds in St Peter's Square (▶ 36–37) from his apartments on Sunday mornings.

Drink coffee: have a really good coffee at Bar Sant'Eustachio (✉ Piazza Sant'Eustachio 82, ☎ 06 6880 2048).

Browse the markets: spend a Sunday morning at Porta Portese flea market or pick your own lunch ingredients at the Campo de'Fiori food market (▶ 134).

Window shop: or buy, in the designer area around Via Condotti (▶ 157–158).

Head to the beach: if you need a break from city life, the nearest beaches are at Ostia, Fregene and Torvaianica.

Eat an ice cream: indulge in a sumptuous *gelato* at Tre Scalini, as you pause to people-watch in Piazza Navona (▶ 52–53).

Watch soccer: join the fans as they cheer on Lazio or AS Roma at the Stadio Olimpico (✉ Via dei Gladiatori ☎ 06 3685 7520).

Best churches

Basilica di Santa Maria Maggiore (► 137), for mosaics.

Il Gesù (► 106), for baroque opulence.

Sant'Andrea al Quirinale (► 147), for Bernini.

San Clemente (► 54–55), for history.

San Giovanni in Laterano (► 87), for history.

Santa Maria in Domnica (► 89), for mosaics.

Santa Maria sopra Minerva (► 124), for art and originality
(a Gothic church, rare for Rome).

Santa Maria del Popolo (► 148–149), for art.

Santa Maria in Trastevere (► 125), for mosaics.

St Peter's (► 36–37), for size, importance and everything else.

Places to take the children

Aquafelix

A water park with an exotic range of themed rides and slides – most children under five may find it a little too much. There are also shops, a bar and a self-service restaurant.

✉ Autostrada Roma–Civitavecchia at the Civitavecchia Nord Exit
☎ 0766 32221 🕐 Jun–Sep daily 10–6

Aquapiper

An outdoor swimming pool complex with a children's pool, another pool with a wave machine and an exciting (or terrifying) slide. Also ponies, camels, a picnic area, a bar and a games room.

✉ Via Maremmana Inferiore Km 29, Guidonia ☎ 0774 326 538
🕐 Jun to first week in Sep daily 9–7 🚌 From Ponte Mammolo to Palombara

Bioparco

Rome's zoo underwent a transformation in the late 1990s to re-emerge as a champion of environmental awareness. Visitors are encouraged to learn more about the natural habitats of the animals and to play an active part in their conservation.

✉ Piazzale del Giardino Zoologico, Villa Borghese ☎ 06 360 8211
🕐 Apr–Sep Mon–Fri 9:30–6, Sat, Sun 9:30–7; Oct daily 9:30–6;
Nov–end Mar Mon–Fri 9:30–5 🚌 To Piazza Ungheria

Castel Sant'Angelo

This atmospheric tomb-cum-fortress-cum-palace has some wonderful *trompe l'oeils* and lots of winding, secret corridors and gloomy guardrooms (➤ 40–41).

Colosseo (Colosseum)
See the corridors through which lions came on their way to eat their unlucky victims (► 42–43).

Explora, Il Museo dei Bambini
Explora is the first museum in Rome aimed at the under 12s. Here they are allowed to touch and play with a range of educational exhibits. Hands-on is the key here.
✉ Via Flaminia 82 ☎ 06 361 3766, www.mdbr.it 🕐 Tue–Sat 9–6:45, Sun 10–6:45 🚌 To Via Flaminia

Luna Park (Luneur)
This 30-year-old funfair is the nearest that Rome gets to a theme park. Most of its attractions are fairly traditional – a hall of mirrors, a ferris wheel, roller-coasters and merry-go-rounds – but recent additions include some more ambitious contraptions.
✉ Via delle Tre Fontane ☎ 592 5933; www.luneur.it 🕐 Telephone for latest opening details 🚇 Magliana 🚌 To Via delle Tre Fontane

Museo delle Cere
The surreality of some of the tableaux may appeal more to adults than to children used to Madame Tussaud's, but it is still worth going to see what Leonardo da Vinci and his contemporaries might have looked like. Around 250 famous personalities in wax.
✉ Piazza dei Santi Apostoli 67 ☎ 06 679 6482; www.museodellacere.it 🕐 9–8 🚌 To Piazza Venezia

Museo della Civiltà Romana
Models of what ancient Rome was really like (► 82).

Museo di Roma in Trastevere
As well as paintings of what Rome looked like when all these artists were strolling around, there are some amusing waxworks

a walk through the historic centre

Combine this walk with visits to the Forum and the Vatican and you can claim to have 'done' Rome.

From Piazza Farnese take Vicolo dei Baulari into Campo de'Fiori (▶ 102), where you can have an early lunch. Go to the far left-hand corner and into Piazza della Cancelleria.

Palazzo della Cancelleria (now Vatican offices) was built between 1485 and 1513 for a great-nephew of the Pope.

Turn right on Corso Vittorio Emanuele II; cross at the lights. Continue down Via Cuccagna into Piazza Navona (▶ 52–53). Halfway up the piazza, Corso Agone leads to Palazzo Madama; Via Salvatore runs alongside, to San Luigi dei Francesi on the left. Continue to the Pantheon.

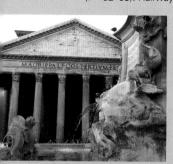

Visit the Pantheon (▶ 50–51), built by Emperor Hadrian in the first century AD, watch the activity or have an expensive coffee.

Take the right-hand alley that is opposite the Pantheon, Vicolo della Maddalena, then turn right down Via del Vicario into the Piazza del Montecitorio. Follow Via di Guglia, in front of the palazzo, then turn left at Via dei Pastini into the Piazza di Pietra.

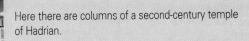

Here there are columns of a second-century temple of Hadrian.

Walk past the columns, down Via di Pietra, cross Via del Corso and continue up Via delle Muratte to the Trevi fountain (▶ 138). Follow Via della Stamperia, right of the fountain, turn right up Via del Tritone, cross and turn left on Via dei Due Macelli to Piazza di Spagna (▶ 146).

Rest by Bernini's Fontana della Barcaccia.

Climb the Spanish Steps, turn left, past Villa Medici, take the path on the right to the Pincio Gardens. Here are wonderful views over Piazza del Popolo (▶ 145).

Distance 4km (2.5 miles) **Time** 3.5 hours with stops, 2 hours without
Start point Piazza Farnese ➕ 15H 🚌 To Corso Vittorio Emanuele II
End point Piazza del Popolo ➕ 7C 🚇 Flaminio
Lunch Hostaria Romanesca (€) ✉ Campo de' Fiori 40 🕐 Tue–Sun

Stunning views

The ramparts of Castel Sant'Angelo (► 40–41)

Colle Oppio (reached after an uphill stroll to Via N Salvi)

Gianicolo (► 107)

Monumento Nazionale a Vittorio Emanuele II (► 80–81)

Palatino (► 82–83)

The rear of Piazza del Campidoglio (near Musei Capitolini, ▶ 46)

Piazza Trinità dei Monti, at the top of the Spanish Steps (▶ 146)

Pincio Gardens, Villa Borghese (▶ 138–139)

Ponte Garibaldi

St Peter's dome (▶ 36–37)

Best museums

Musei Capitolini: Features some of the most famous statues of Roman antiquity (➤ 46–47).

Musei Vaticani: An enormous collection of art, sculpture and other artefacts accumulated by the papacy over the centuries (➤ 38–39, 162–169).

Palazzo Altemps: A sublime collection of Roman sculpture in a beautiful palace setting (➤ 142).

Palazzo Barberini: This rambling palace houses a large state collection of paintings and other medieval and Renaissance treasures (➤ 48–49).

Palazzo Corsini: A sister gallery to the Palazzo Barberini, with paintings from leading 16th- and 17th-century artists (➤ 112).

Palazzo Doria Pamphilj: A private art collection with innumerable masterpices in one of Rome's most sumptuous palaces (➤ 113).

Palazzo Massimo alle Terme: The city's finest array of Roman and Greek mosaics, paintings and sculpture (➤ 142–143).

Palazzo Spada: A small but exquisite collection of medieval art and Roman sculpture in a palace partly designed by Borromini (➤ 116).

Palazzo Venezia: The city's most important collection of medieval decorative arts (➤ 117).

Villa Giulia: A large museum devoted to the art and culture of the Etruscans (➤ 151).

Exploring

Rome has been a major city for longer than most other European capitals have existed. First the heart of the Roman Empire, a few centuries later it emerged as the centre of the Roman Catholic faith and in 1870 it became the capital of the newly united Italy. Museums here house artworks and artefacts from well over 2,000 years of history – ancient sculptures, delicate early Renaissance and opulent baroque paintings all vie for the viewer's attention.

The city itself is a joy to explore: major monuments, museums and churches are found on every corner, and wherever you look you are likely to come across picturesque details (balconies festooned with flowers and washing, sleepy cats snoozing on cars, ruined splendour, small shrines with portraits of the Madonna) that are guaranteed to charm and delight. Stop off in a piazza for a *caffè* and *gelato* – this is the *dolce vita*!

The Ancient City and the South

What remains of ancient Rome is not confined to a single area of the modern city. Buildings and monuments from the era of empire and earlier are scattered far and wide, yet the heart of the old city – around the Capitoline, Palatine and Esquiline hills – still has the largest present-day concentration of ancient monuments.

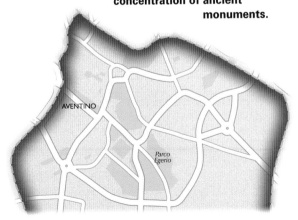

ARCO DI COSTANTINO

Although it is known as Constantine's Arch, scholars now believe that this magnificent monument outside the Colosseum was built for the emperor Trajan, and adopted by Constantine, who rededicated it to his own triumph over co-emperor Maxentius in AD315. In any event, many of the carved panels and medallions were scavenged from older monuments, including the figures of Dacian prisoners at the top of the columns, which were almost certainly carved for Trajan.

🕂 19J ⊠ Piazza del Colosseo 🖐 Free 🚇 Colosseo 🚌 60, 75, 85, 87, 117, 175 to Piazza del Colosseo

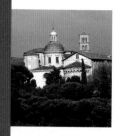

BASILICA DI SANTI GIOVANNI E PAOLO

Archaeology meets legend in this church, built over a Roman house and containing Roman and medieval frescoes (seen by appointment only). Saints John and Paul were martyred here in AD362, and their bodies, discovered only in the 20th century, are now in an ancient porphyry urn under the altar. The inside was re-modelled in 1718. There is a 13th-century fresco in a small room near the altar that depicts Christ and his Apostles. The church itself is predominantly Byzantine and has one of the most beautiful belltowers in Rome (1150), which was added by the only English pope, Nicholas Breakspear (Adrian IV), as well as a majestic portico incorporating ancient columns.

🕂 19K ⊠ Piazza dei Santi Giovanni e Paolo 13 ☎ 06 7005 745 🕓 Daily 8:30–12, 3–6:30. Closed during services 🚇 Colosseo 🚌 81, 673 to Via della Navicella

BASILICA DI SAN PAOLO FUORI LE MURA

Built on the site of St Paul's execution (*c* AD67), the present basilica dates from 1874 (Poletti), the original (*c* AD386–410) having burnt down in 1823. The only surviving parts are in the transept, the bronze doors (1070), an impressive example of a paschal candlestick (*c*1190), Arnolfo di Cambio's lovely Gothic *baldacchino* (1285) and the beautiful cloisters (1205–41), with their lavishly decorated mosaic columns (1214, Vassallettis). The general tone, however, is somewhat heavy-handed and 19th-century.
www.abbaziasanpaolo.net

✠ 17M (off map) ✉ Via Ostiense 186 ☎ 06 4543 5574 ⊘ Daily 7–7; cloisters 9–1, 3–6 Ⓜ San Paolo 🚌 128, 761, 770 to San Paolo Basilica

BASILICA DI SAN SEBASTIANO

The basilica dates from the first half of the fifth century, on the spot where Peter and Paul's bodies were allegedly buried (their names can be seen in the graffiti on the walls of the catacombs beneath). The present building dates from the early 17th century. The burial chambers (entered on the left of the façade) also contain exquisite Roman frescoes and stucco work. In pride of place, however, is the crypt of St Sebastian, whose image, pierced by the Diocletian guards' arrows, was particularly popular during the Renaissance. His body lies in the calm white-walled basilica above.

✚ 21M (off map) ✉ Via Appia Antica 136 ☎ 06 780 8847 ⏰ Mon–Sat 8:30–12, 2:30–5:30 🚌 118, 660 to San Sebastiano

CARCERE MAMERTINO (MAMERTINE PRISON)

This dank, dark dungeon dates from the fourth century BC and was where any potential threats to state security, including the leaders of opposing armies, were thrown to starve to death (their bodies were dropped into the main sewer, the Cloaca Maxima). St Peter is said to have been imprisoned here before being crucified and an altar has been built next to the spring that he miraculously created in order to christen other prisoners and two of his guards.

✚ 18H ✉ Clivo Argentario 1, Via di San Pietro in Carcere ☎ 06 679 2902 ⏰ Apr–end Sep 9–12, 2–6:30; Oct–end Mar 9–12:30, 2:30–5 ✋ Donation 🚌 44, 46, 84, 715, 716, 780, 781, 810, 916 to Piazza Venezia

CATACOMBE DI SAN CALLISTO

In ancient Rome, when Christianity was still very much a minority religion, it was against the law to bury the dead within the city confines. The catacombs of San Callisto, set in rolling parkland off the Via Appia Antica, are among the largest and most visited. Here there are an estimated 20km (12 miles) of underground galleries on four levels lined with niches, or *loculi,* cut into the rock in which the shrouded bodies of the dead were laid to rest behind stone. Many of the early popes were buried here. The guided tours (offered in a range of languages, including English, French and German) cover about 1km (0.5 miles).

www.catacombe.roma.it

✚ 21M (off map) ✉ Via Appia Antica 110 ☎ 06 5130 1580 🕐 Thu–Tue 8:30–12, 2:30–5:30 (5 in winter); closed Feb ✋ Moderate 🚌 118, 660 to San Callisto

CIMITERO PROTESTANTE (PROTESTANT CEMETERY)

This serene spot was officially called the non-Catholic, rather than the Protestant, cemetery, but in the first years after its establishment in 1738 most of its occupants were Protestant and the name has stuck. A map at the entrance will help you locate the final resting places of, among others, English poets Keats and Shelley, Julius, the son of German poet J. W. von Goethe, and Antonio Gramsci, the founder of the Italian Communist Party.

✚ 17M ✉ Via Caio Cestio 6 🕐 Tue–Sat 9–5, Sun 9–2, but subject to change without notice ✋ Donation 🚌 3, 23, 60, 75, 118, 280 to Via Marmorata or Piazza di Porta San Paolo

CIRCO MASSIMO

There is not much of this ancient racetrack left but you can make out the tight oval that the charioteers raced round and the sloped side on which there seating for up to 300,000 spectators. The remains of that seating can still be seen at the circus's southern end, although the tower there is medieval. Chariot races were held here from the fourth century BC until they went out of fashion in the sixth century. The site was also used for animal fights, mock sea battles (for which it was flooded), athletics and executions.

🕂 18K 🖂 Via del Circo Massimo 🖐 Free 🚇 Circo Massimo 🚌 60, 75, 160, 175, 628, 673 to Piazza di Porta Capena

COLOSSEO

Best places to see, ➤ 42–43.

DOMUS AUREA

The Domus Aurea is Emperor Nero's 'Golden House'. After the great fire of AD64 destroyed over half the city, Nero built this huge

symbol of imperial power over the ruins. It is adorned with elegant fresco cycles and paintings. The Domus Aurea is currently closed for restoration. When it reopens, bear in mind that you need to reserve tickets in advance.

🕂 20H 🖂 Via della Domus Aurea, Colle Oppio 🕿 06 3996 7700 🕐 Closed for restoration

🖐 Moderate 🚇 Colosseo 🚌 60, 75, 84, 85, 87, 117, 175, 810, 850 to Colosseo

FORI IMPERIALI

Opposite and next to the main Roman Forum (➤ 44–45) lie the remaining fragments of five other, smaller forums, each built by an

emperor to accommodate the overspill when the original forum became too small to cope with the demands of an expanding empire. To the right of the main entrance to the Roman Forum, underneath the Vittorio Emanuele Monument (➤ 80–81), is the oldest of these, built by Julius Caesar in 51BC. On the other side of the wide avenue that Mussolini built over other ancient remains to act as a triumphal route up to his Palazzo Venezia headquarters (➤ 117) are the remains of the forums of Trajan (Mercati Traiani ➤ 80), Augustus (where you can see some fine columns and friezes), Vespasian and Nerva.

🚼 18H 🖂 Via dei Fori Imperiali ☎ 06 679 0048 🕔 Call ahead to reserve tickets and find out opening times 💷 Expensive 🚇 Colosseo 🚌 60, 84, 85, 87, 117, 175, 810, 850 to Via dei Fori Imperiali

FORO ROMANO
Best places to see, ➤ 44–45.

MERCATI TRAIANI

Emperor Trajan commissioned this five-level complex of about 150 small shops from the Greek architect Apollodorus of Damascus in the early second century AD, making it one of the first shopping malls in the world.

Goods from all over the empire were sold here and shops were probably arranged by area – storage jars found on the first floor suggest that wine and oil were sold here, while fruit and flower shops probably occupied the ground floor. The finely carved column next to the markets was erected in AD113 to celebrate Trajan's campaigns in Dacia (Romania). It is 40m (131ft) high and originally bore a statue of the emperor, which was replaced by the present statue of St Peter in 1587.

✚ 18G ✉ Via IV Novembre 94 ☎ 06 679 0048 ✪ Closed for restoration ✋ Expensive 🚌 40, 60, 64, 70, 117, 170 to Via IV Novembre

MONUMENTO A VITTORIO EMANUELE II

A monument of many names; il Vittoriale was built at the end of the 19th century to honour the first king of the united Italy, whose

equestrian statue stands out proudly in front. Behind him burns the eternal flame, guarded day and night by armed soldiers at the Altar of the Nation. Other, less complimentary, ways of referring to this colonnaded mass of white marble include the 'typewriter' and the 'wedding cake'. In any event, you cannot miss it.

🕇 18H ✉ Piazza Venezia ☎ 06 699 1718 ⏱ Apr–end Sep 9:30–5:30, Oct–end Mar 9:30–4:30 ✋ Free 🚌 44, 46, 84, 715, 716, 780, 781, 810, 916 to Piazza Venezia

MUSEI CAPITOLINI
Best places to see, ➤ 46–47.

MUSEO DELL'ALTO MEDIOEVO
This museum houses decorative arts of the fifth to eleventh centuries (from the fall of the Roman Empire to the Renaissance). Most of the items were found locally, and include some beautiful jewellery from the seventh century, fragments of elaborate embroidery from clerical robes and a delicate fifth-century gold fibula (a brooch used to fasten clothing) found on the Palatine hill. Swords made from gold and silver, intricately carved and decorated, have clearly withstood the test of time.

🕇 20M (off map) ✉ Viale Lincoln 3, EUR ☎ 06 5422 8199 ⏱ Tue–Sun 9–8 ✋ Inexpensive 🚇 Magliana 🚌 714, 715 to Piazzale G. Marconi

MUSEO DELLE ARTI E TRADIZIONI POPOLARI
A huge collection of fascinating objects relating to Italian folk art and rural traditions. On display are agricultural and pastoral tools, including elaborately decorated carts and horse tack, artisan instruments and handiwork, clothing, furniture, musical instruments, some exquisite traditional jewellery and photographs documenting how the exhibits were used.

www.popolari.arti.benicultural.it

🕇 20M (off map) ✉ Piazza G. Marconi 8, EUR ☎ 06 592 6148 ⏱ Tue–Sat 9–6, Sun and public hols 9–8 ✋ Inexpensive 🚇 Magliana 🚌 714, 715

MUSEO DELLA CIVILTÀ ROMANA

The models inside this building give a sense of what life was like in ancient Rome and help put into context the fragments and artefacts that are the treasures of so many of the city's museums. There are busts and statues of the key figures of the day, reproductions of Roman furniture, surgical tools, musical instruments and sundials. The highlight is a giant scale model of Rome in the fourth century AD, at the time of Constantine, showing every building within the circular Aurelian walls.

www.comune.roma.it/museociviltaroma

✚ 20M (off map) ✉ Piazza Gianni Agnelli 10, EUR ☎ 06 592 6041 🕐 Tue–Fri 9–2, Sat, Sun 9–7 💰 Expensive 🚇 Magliana 🚌 714, 715 to Piazza G. Marconi

PALATINO

Attached to the Forum (admission includes both), this is a peaceful, lush, hilly area covered with the remains of the massive palaces that the Roman emperors built for themselves. Most of what is on view dates from the first century AD. It can be frustrating to visit because many of the main attractions close at short notice and little is labelled, but there are guaranteed views of the Forum (▶ 44–45) from the delightful semi-formal Orti Farnesiani (Farnese Gardens), laid out in the 16th century. Underneath the gardens is a long tunnel built by Nero and decorated with stucco reliefs, some of which have survived. He may

have intended this as a promenade for hot weather although some researchers believe that it led all the way to his massive palace overlooking the spot where the Colosseum stands today. Other highlights of the Palatine include the baths of Septimus Severus, the wall paintings in the house of Livia and traces of an eighth-century BC village of huts.

🕂 18J ✉ Through the Forum or Via di San Gregorio ☎ 06 3996 7700
🕐 Daily 9–1 hour before sunset ✋ Expensive; tickets also valid for Colosseo
🚇 Colosseo 🚌 60, 75, 85, 87, 117, 175, 810 to Via di San Gregorio

PALAZZO COLONNA

Some of the most beautiful ceiling frescoes in Rome adorn this palace's opulent 18th-century galleries. There are some fine portraits in the first room, but the eye automatically wanders through to the lavishly gilded Great Hall, with its magnificent ceiling painting representing the life of Marcantonio Colonna. As you step down take care not to trip over the cannonball, which became lodged there during the siege of Rome in 1849. Two ornate cabinets – one with inlaid carved ivory panels reproducing works by Raphael and Michelangelo (the central panel is his *Last Judgement* from the Sistine Chapel) – give the Room of the Desks its name. The Apotheosis of the Colonna Pope Martin V decorates the ceiling of the fourth room, where Annibale Caracci's *Bean Eater* makes an amusing change from more serious subjects. In the Throne Room a chair is kept ready (turned to the wall) in case of a papal visit.

www.galleriacolonna.it

✚ 8F ✉ Via della Pilotta 17 ☎ 06 678 4350 ⏰ Sep–end Jul Sat 9–1
✋ Expensive 🚌 44, 46, 84, 715, 716, 780, 781, 810, 916 to Piazza Venezia

PIAZZA DEI CAVALIERI DI MALTA

Piranesi, famous for his surreal etchings of Roman views, designed this peaceful piazza in 1765 and decorated it with the symbols and devices of the Order of the Knights of Malta, whose priory is here. In the door of the priory is a peephole that offers a magnificent miniature view of the dome of St Peter's, seen beyond the tree-lined avenue of the priory's garden. This part of the city, the Aventine, has always been a genteel residential area.

✚ 17K ✉ Piazza dei Cavalieri di Malta 🚌 23, 30, 44, 95, 170, 280, 716, 781 to Lungotevere Aventino

PIRAMIDE CESTIA

An engineer could tell you that this is not nearly as well built as the Egyptian originals that inspired magistrate Caius Cestis (in Italian, Caio Cestio) when he was designing his own tomb in the 1st century BC – a time when the fashion for all things Egyptian was at its height. For all that, this 27m (89ft) high pyramid has stood the test of time and makes a somewhat surreal landmark next to the Porta San Paolo, one of the original gateways into Rome.

✚ 17M ✉ Piazzale Ostiense
🚇 Piramide 🚌 3, 60, 75, 118, 715 to Piramide

PORTA SAN SEBASTIANO

The best-preserved of Rome's ancient gateways, the Porto San Sebastiano, leading to the Via Appia Antica, was rebuilt in the fifth century AD. Today it houses a rather dry museum on the history of the Roman city walls, the highlight of which is a stretch of walkway along the top of the third-century AD Aurelian wall.

✚ 21M (off map) ✉ Via di Porta San Sebastiano 18 ☎ 06 7047 5284
🕐 Tue–Sat 9–7, Sun 9–2 ✋ Inexpensive 🚌 218, 660 to Porta San Sebastiano

SAN CLEMENTE

Best places to see, ➤ 54–55.

SANTA CROCE IN GERUSALEMME

This church bursts with relics; indeed it was built (1144) for that very purpose. In the Chapel of the Relics are pieces of the True Cross and thorns from Christ's Crown brought to Rome by the Empress Helena in AD320, whose crypt is built on soil from Mount Golgotha. The chapel contains wonderfully ornamental mosaics showing scenes decked with flowers and birds.

✚ 24J ✉ Piazza di Santa Croce in Gerusalemme ☎ 06 701 4769
🕐 Daily 7–7, but hours may vary
🚌 117, 186, 218, 650, 850 to Piazza Santa Croce in Gerusalemme

SAN GIOVANNI IN LATERANO

This was the home of the papacy from the time of Constantine until 1305, and is the present cathedral of Rome. In short, it is an important place. The early buildings suffered from fire and neglect after the pope was exiled to Avignon and the subsequent move to the Vatican. The present-

day San Giovanni dates from the baroque: including Fontana's palace and portico (1585), Gallei's façade and Borromini's nave

(1650), which includes the columns of the original basilica inside a new and vigorous structure, creating niches for figures of the Apostles. Look for the fifth-century mosaics in the baptistery apse and the bronze door (1190) of the chapel of St John the Evangelist. The baptistery was damaged by a bomb in 1993.

✚ 22K ✉ Piazza di San Giovanni in Laterano ☎ 06 6988 6433 ⑤ Church daily 7–6. Cloisters daily 9–12, 4–6. Baptistery daily 9–12, 4–7 ⓜ San Giovanni 🚌 3, 6, 85, 87, 117, 850 to Piazza di San Giovanni in Laterano

SAN GREGORIO MAGNO

Originally Gregory the Great's monastery (AD575), from where he set out to take Christianity to England, it is now a feast of baroque, with Soria's masterpiece of a façade (1629) sitting decorously at the top of a splendid flight of stairs. More interesting than the church interior is the adjacent Oratory. The first room contains the table (supported by third-century carved griffins) from which Gregory was said to have fed 12 poor people daily. In the central chapel (dedicated to St Andrew) is the lovely misty-hued fresco by Reni of *St Andrew Adoring the Cross* and Domenichino's even lovelier *Scourging*.

🞤 19K 🖂 Piazza di San Gregorio Magno ☎ 06 700 9357 🕓 Daily 9–12, 3–6 🚇 Circo Massimo 🚌 81, 117, 118, 628, 673 to Via di San Gregorio

SANTA MARIA IN COSMEDIN

The austere intimacy of this lovingly restored 12th-century basilica in the heart of ancient Rome makes a wonderful setting for the beautiful cosmati works so characteristic of Roman churches of the period. The Cosmati (actually several families but grouped together because of the preponderance of the name Cosma) were builders and designers but are best remembered for their luscious decorations in marble and colourful mosaics. Examples can be seen here in the magnificent nave paving (1123), the raised choir, the paschal candlestick, the bishop's throne and, in particular, the beautiful *baldacchino* (1294). In the portico is the *Bocca della Verità* (mouth of truth) – legend has it that the mouth would bite the hand of he who lied – or more commonly she whose marital fidelity was questioned. In the sacristy are mosaics (AD706) from old St Peter's.

✚ 17J ✉ Piazza della Bocca della Verità 18 ☎ 06 678 1419 🕐 Daily 9–1, 2–7 (6 in winter) 🚌 30, 44, 950 to Piazza della Bocca della Verità

SANTA MARIA IN DOMNICA

A haven of calm, this lovely church was rebuilt (AD817–24) in honour of the Virgin (who takes pride of place in the delightful apse mosaic showing saints striding through meadows). It is also known as *La Navicella* on account of the 16th-century copy of a Roman boat in front of the entrance. The boat is a fountain, made from an ancient stone galley; this may have been an offering made by a safely returned traveller. Pope Leo X added the portico and the ceiling. The theme of journeying continues in the 12 images of great delicacy and simplicity on the 11th-century wooden ceiling (among which are the ark, the tree of life and, in the middle, the Medici coat of arms). There is a notable ninth-century mosaic in the apse, which was commissioned by Pope Paschal I. Some excavated Roman remains are exhibited under the altar.

✚ 20K ✉ Piazza della Navicella 10 ☎ 06 700 1519 🕐 Daily 9–12, 3:30–6 Ⓜ Colosseo 🚌 81, 673 to Via della Navicella

a walk from the Celian Hill

The green and peaceful Celian Hill overlooks the Colosseum and adjoins the Baths of Caracalla and the Circo Massimo.

Starting at San Gregorio Magno (➤ 88), turn right up Via di San Gregorio and take the first right, Clivo di Scauro, which runs under the flying buttresses that support the Basilica di Santi Giovanni e Paolo (➤ 74). Continue straight up Via di San Paolo della Croce, under the first-century Arch of Dolabella and past the gateway of San Tommaso in Formis.

San Tommaso in Formis has a 13th-century mosaic of Christ freeing a black and a white slave. To the left is the church of Santo Stefano Rotondo (➤ 94), and on the right is Santa Maria in Domnica (➤ 89); the fountain was erected in 1931 using a 16th-century sculpture of a boat. Next to the church is the entrance to Villa Celimontana park.

At the bottom of Via della Navicella bear right down Via Druso and turn right along Viale delle Terme di Caracalla, passing the baths (➤ 94–95) to reach the Circo Massimo (➤ 78).

Rest on the grass here and let your imagination drift back to the chariot races, which were cheered on by up to 300,000 spectators.

Turn left on Viale Aventino and take the first right up Via del Circo Massimo. Follow this to Piazzale Ugo La Malfa and take the second left, Via di Valle Murcia, following it up to the top .

Here there is a small orange garden with views over Rome. Following Via di Santa Sabina you reach Santa Sabina (➤ 93) and Santi Bonifacio e Alessio, with its 18th-century façade, cosmati doorway and belltower.

Continue straight to Piazza dei Cavalieri di Malta (➤ 85). Turning left just before the piazza down Via di Porta Lavernale will take you back down to Via Marmorata for buses, but first have lunch near Piramide.

Distance 4km (2.5 miles) **Time** 3 hours with stops, 2 hours without
Start point San Gregorio Magno ✚ 19K 🚇 Circo Massimo
🚌 To Circo Massimo or Piazza del Colosseo
End point Via Marmorata ✚ 17M 🚇 Piramide
🚌 To Via Marmorata
Lunch Taverna Cestia (€€) ✉ Viale della Piramide Cestia 87
☎ 06 574 3754 🕐 Tue–Sun 🚇 Piramide
🚌 3, 60, 75, 118, 715 to Piramide

SAN PIETRO IN VINCOLI

To appreciate Michelangelo's *Moses* without jostling for position in front of the memorial to Julius II, make an early start. Flanked by Leah and Rachel (ironically representing contemplation), Moses remains remarkably impervious to the clicking cameras and rustling guidebooks, his gaze reaching out to some indeterminate spot across the nave, his hands sagaciously pulling back his abundant beard. Sculpted from a single piece of Carrara marble between 1513 and 1516, Moses is built on a large scale, with enormous legs weighing him down and exquisitely moulded musculature; he is a massive expression of power and strength. Nearby, under the altar, lie St Peter's chains.

✝ 20H ✉ Piazza San Pietro in Vincoli 4a
☎ 06 488 2865 🕐 Daily 9–12, 3–6 (hours may vary) Ⓜ Cavour, Colosseo 🚌 75, 84 to Via Cavour

SANTI QUATTRO CORONATI

Make sure you ask to visit the Oratory of St Silvester, with its delightful frescoes (1246), *Scenes from the Life of Constantine*, in the adjoining convent. In soothing faded hues, and proof of how persistent was the influence of Byzantine art in Rome, you can see poor, spotty Constantine being cured of the pox by Pope Silvester. On the ceiling is a unique cross of five majolica plates. The Chapel of Santa Barbara has remains of medieval frescoes, and there is a garden in the inner courtyard. The church of Santi Quattro Coronati (Four Crowned Saints) has a typically complicated history; originally fourth-century, it was rebuilt in the 12th, as you can see from the belltower and cosmati paving.

🔂 21J 🖂 Via dei Santi Quattro Coronati 20 ☎ 06 7047 5427 ⊗ Church daily 6:30–12, 3:30–7. Oratory and cloisters Mon–Sat 10–12, 4:30–6, Sun 4:30–6 🚌 3, 85, 117, 218, 650, 850 to Via San Giovanni in Laterano

SANTA SABINA

The light-bathed interior of this perfect, serene early Christian basilica was built for Peter of Illyria (AD422–32). The belltower and cloisters were added in 1218, when the church was given to St Dominic and his newly formed order. Dominic's orange tree can be peeked at through a small gap in the

portico. The church is named after the Roman Sabina, martyred in Hadrian's time. Inside, the beautifully proportioned antique columns, with their delicately carved Corinthian capitals, support the nave arcading and fifth-century frieze. Unfortunately, the fifth-century mosaics on the apse and arch have not survived; the fresco reproductions are 15th-century.

🔂 17K 🖂 Piazza Pietro d'Illiria 1 ☎ 06 5794 0600 ⊗ Daily 7–12:30, 3:30–7 🚌 3, 60, 73 75, 118, to Viale Aventino; 175 to Lungotevere Aventino

SANTO STEFANO ROTONDO

Santo Stefano is one of the oldest round churches in Rome,
c AD470, and has a contemplative ambience. Originally, the outer
walls were farther out, with circular and cross-shaped windows,
and there were eight entrances. No evidence of an altar has been
found (the present one is 13th-century); the two central columns
supporting the lofty white-washed dome are also later additions.
To the left of the present-day entrance, a section of the original
flooring has been painstakingly recreated using excavated marble
fragments. Faded representations of gruesome martyrdoms (by
Pomerancio and others, *c*1600) adorn the walls.

✝ 20K ✉ Via di Santa Stefano 7 ☎ 06 481 9333 🕐 Closed for restoration
🚌 81, 673 to Via della Navicella

TERME DI CARACALLA

Ancient Romans did not go to the baths just to keep clean but also
to relax, meet each other, discuss politics, exercise and even
study. Even bathing itself was not merely a soak in a tub; the

Romans started off with a sauna, followed by a scrape down, a hot bath, a tepid bath and, finally, a dive into the cold bath. The serene ruins of the baths that Caracalla built in the third century AD include remains of each of these types of bath, as well as gyms, a library and a complicated underfloor heating system. They are used for summer outdoor opera performances.

✠ 20L ✉ Via delle Terme di Caracalla 52 ☎ 06 3996 7700; book online at www.pierreci.it 🕐 Tue–Sun 9 to 1 hour before sunset, Mon 9–2 💰 Moderate 🚇 Circo Massimo 🚌 60, 75, 81, 175, 673 to Via delle Terme di Caracalla

TESTACCIO

Although well-known to Romans, who flock to its traditional restaurants and less-traditional nightclubs in the evenings, the Testaccio area is off the main tourist track. Most of its buildings are tall, courtyarded residential blocks, dating from the end of the 19th century and designed to include schools, crèches and shops. It is the area around Monte Testaccio that sees the action, especially at night and during the summer. The *monte* is made up of millions of broken *amphorae*, dumped here by ancient Roman dockers when this was the port area, where ships unloaded their cargo, including the oil that was transported in these clay pots. Opposite the hill is the old *mattatoio* – the

most sophisticated abattoir in Europe when it opened in 1891. Now it's used for concerts, exhibitions and other cultural events.

✠ 16L ✉ Area between Via Marmorata and Lungotevere Testaccio 🚌 3, 23, 30, 75, 280, 716 to Via Marmorata; 95, 170, 781 to Lungotevere Testaccio

HOTELS

Celio (€€)

The three-star Celio is pleasantly small (just 19 rooms) and is in a reasonably quiet street that is nevertheless well situated for the Colosseum. The rooms are comfortable and tasteful.

✉ Via Santissimi Quattro 35c ☎ 06 7049 5333; www.hotelcelio.com

Ⓜ Colosseo 🚌 To Piazza del Colosseo or Via di San Giovanni in Laterano

Perugia (€)

Perugia is modest with no frills, but the multi-lingual staff are friendly and most of the 11 rooms have bathrooms. It is two steps from the Colosseum.

✉ Via del Colosseo 7 ☎ 06 679 7200; www.hperugia.it Ⓜ Colosseo

🚌 To Via Cavour, Colosseo

Sant'Anselmo (€€)

A lovely, reasonably priced hotel in a villa with garden in the heart of ancient Rome. There are wheelchair facilities.

✉ Piazza Sant'Anselmo 2 ☎ 06 570 057; www.aventinohotels.com

Ⓜ Circo Massimo 🚌 To Via Aventino

Shangri la' Corsetti (€€)

Found outside of the central district, with every amenity, including a good restaurant.

✉ Viale Algeria 141 ☎ 06 591 6441; www. shangrilacorsetti.it

Ⓜ EUR Fermi 🚌 To Palazzo dello Sporto

RESTAURANTS

Binario 4 (€)

A welcome arrival near the Colosseum, Binario 4 is an updated version of the genuine local *osteria*. There are carefully executed traditional dishes itemized daily on a strategically placed blackboard. Expect informal bonhomie. There are no rules on how many courses you need to eat – have as little or as much as you like. An added bonus is that the place stays open until late.

✉ Via San Giovanni in Laterano 32 ☎ 06 700 5561 🕐 Wed–Mon, Tue dinner only Ⓜ Colosseo 🚌 To Piazza del Colosseo

Cecilia Metella (€€)

At the top of a winding drive, Cecilia Metella has tables in a delightful garden setting, complete with fountain. There's a large, open-fire interior for winter. Cheerful, bustling waiters. Stress-free parking.

✉ Via Appia Antica 125–129 ☎ 06 513 6743 🕔 Tue–Sun 🚌 118

Checchino dal 1887 (€€€)

In the heart of Testaccio, this cool vaulted restaurant vaunts the experience of more than 100 years. The quintessential Roman cuisine is based on the once lowly offerings from the old slaughterhouse opposite. A superb natural wine cellar complements the meal.

✉ Via di Monte Testaccio 30 ☎ 06 574 6318 🕔 Tue–Sat 🚇 Piramide 🚌 3, 60, 75, 118

Hostaria Antica Roma (€€€)

A pleasant stop on the Appian Way and attractively illuminated by candlelight for dinner. Specialties include *gnocchi* with clams, fillet of bass with herbs and beef fillet with truffles. A 2,000-year-old recipe is used for the flan cake. Other ancient Roman dishes are a feature on Tuesdays and Thursdays.

✉ Via Appia Antica 87 ☎ 06 513 2888 🕔 Tue–Sun 🚌 118

Nerone (€–€€)

Close to the Colosseum, this small, friendly trattoria is a pleasant spot for an inexpensive and relaxed meal. The *antipasti* is especially good, to be followed by Roman and Abruzzese dishes. A few tables for outside dining.

✉ Via delle Terme di Tito 96 ☎ 06 481 7952 🕔 Mon–Sat 🚌 To Piazza del Colosseo

Pasquilino (€€)

This long-established trattoria is only a few minutes' walk east of the Colosseum and serves large portions of good simple food.

✉ Via dei Santissimi Quattro 66 ☎ 06 700 4576 🕔 Tue–Sun. Closed two weeks in Aug 🚇 Colosseo 🚌 To Piazza del Colosseo

Perilli a Testaccio (€€)

A popular, noisy and crowded trattoria that makes no concessions to fashionable décor and thrives on its reputation for gargantuan portions of honest Roman dishes. Locals rub shoulders with the famous and everybody enjoys themselves. Reservations essential.

✉ Via Marmorata 39 ☎ 06 574 2415 🕐 Thu–Tue 🚇 Piramide 🚌 To Via Marmorata

Li Rioni (€)

An original street-like pizzeria, complete with tiled courtyard, streetlights and balconies. The atmosphere plus the excellent choice of pizzas have made it a local hot spot. It's very popular, so be prepared to stand in line.

✉ Via dei Santissimi Quattro 24 ☎ 06 7045 0605 🕐 Wed–Mon 🚌 To Piazza del Colosseo

Romolo nel Giardino della San Teodoro (€€)

Stumble across this enticing and elegant little trattoria in its romantic setting and you will be treated to a memorable experience, especially in summer. Grilled meats, fresh fish and Roman specialties. Informal and welcoming, with good wines.

✉ Via dei Fienili 49 ☎ 06 678 0933 🕐 Mon–Sat 🚌 To Piazza Bocca della Verità

Taverna Cestia (€€)

A quality-for-money restaurant popular with many of the foreign residents working for the nearby UN agency. An extensive menu of Italian dishes, along with crisp Roman pizzas. Terrace outside.

✉ Viale Piramide Cestia 67 ☎ 06 574 3754 🕐 Tue–Sun 🚇 Piramide 🚌 11, 13, 27, 30

Trattoria Priscilla (€)

A useful place after trekking around the catacombs and one that is not hard on the pocket. Priscilla is a simple family-run trattoria offering classic Roman fare with no concessions to *haute cuisine* but happy to serve a good plate of pasta and a glass of wine.

✉ Via Appia Antica 68 ☎ 06 513 6379 🕐 Mon–Sat 🚌 118

SHOPPING

BOOKS
Bookshop Electa
A museum bookshop on Capitoline Hill, Electa sells museum guides, mythological and historical literature, plus artefacts and artwork, all at reasonable prices.
✉ Piazza del Campidoglio ☎ 06 3996 7800 🚌 To Piazza Venezia

MARKETS
Via Sannio
Popular with Romans for new and second-hand clothes. The leather jackets are excellent value and the shoe stands are good. There are some real bargains in the piles at the back.
✉ Via Sannio 🚇 San Giovanni 🚌 To Via Appia Nuova

Vittorio Emanuele
The largest food market in Rome, also the cheapest, has often been criticized for lowering the tone of this splendid piazza. But it is now under cover in the vast former barracks of Ex-Caserma Sani nearby. There is a wonderful array of fish, fruit and vegetables.
✉ Ex-Caserma Sani di Piazza Vittorio 🚇 Vittorio 🚌 To Piazza Vittorio Emanuele II

ENTERTAINMENT

THEATRE AND DANCE
Colosseo
One of the best venues for seeing works by young Italian directors and playwrights.
✉ Via Capo d'Africa 5a ☎ 06 700 4932; www.teatrocolosseo.it 🚇 Colosseo
🚌 85

MUSIC
Alpheus
Alpheus has three separate areas: one catering for jazz, one for rock and the other for dancing.
✉ Via del Commercio 36 ☎ 06 574 7826; www.alpheus.it 🚇 Piramide
🚌 To Via Ostiense

Palalottomatica

Rome's largest music venue is in the 1960 Olympic Piazzale dello Sport. Big international names have appeared here, such as the Rolling Stones, and top acts continue to come. There are also eight restaurants and numerous bars, and various festivals are held here.

✉ Piazzale dello Sport ☎ 199 128800 🚇 EUR Palasport

NIGHTLIFE
Alibi

A hetero-friendly gay club in the throbbing Testaccio area.

✉ Via di Monte Testaccio 44 ☎ 06 574 3448 🚇 Piramide 🚌 To Via Marmorata

Caffè Latino

One of the earliest of the Testaccio clubs to open. In spite of its name, you're as likely to hear jazz, blues or rock music as you are Latin American. There are usually live acts on Monday, Tuesday and Wednesday.

✉ Via di Monte Testaccio 96 ☎ 06 5728 8556 🚇 Piramide 🚌 To Via Marmorata

Goa

This is one of Rome's trendiest and most stylish nightclubs. Inspired by Southeast Asia, Goa is a cool place to hang out and it attracts some of Europe's top DJs. House, hip-hop, jungle and tribal music predominate. Credit cards are not accepted and the club is closed on Monday.

✉ Via Giuseppe Libetta 13 ☎ 06 574 8277 🚌 To Via Ostiense

SPORT
Ippodromo delle Capannelle

This is Rome's horse-racing track, hosting flat racing, steeplechases and show jumping. Races are held from September to June.

✉ Via Appia Nuova 1255 (off map, east of Piazza dei Re di Roma) ☎ 06 718 8750; www.capannelleippodromo.it 🚌 To Via Appia Nuova

The Heart of Rome

The heart of Rome – the area bounded by the curve of the Tiber in the west and Via del Corso in the east – is often described as 'Renaissance Rome' or 'Baroque Rome' or even 'Medieval Rome'. No description is quite right, for the area is a mixture of ancient monuments, churches, palaces, streets and squares that span some 2,000 years of history.

CAMPO DE'FIORI

Since Renaissance times, this has been one of the busiest and most bustling squares in central Rome and it's still a great place to drop by at any time of day. Many of the old, crumbling buildings have been restored but the fascinatingly precarious many-layered Palazzo Pio Righetti, set at the square's northeastern corner, still looks as though one of its plant-covered balconies may be about to drop off. During the morning there is a lively food market, which packs up noisily as people saunter to the outdoor restaurants and bars at lunchtime. The foreboding, hooded figure in the middle of the piazza is Giordano Bruno, a philosopher who was burnt at the stake here in 1600 for heresy – the statue was erected when the popes lost their political control of Rome at Italian Unification. The maze of narrow streets that surround the piazza are full of carpenters' and jewellers' workshops, as well as antiques shops and second-hand clothing stores.

15G 🖂 Piazza Campo de'Fiori 🚌 40, 46, 62, 64 to Corso Vittorio Emanuele II

CHIESA NUOVA

This was one of the churches that helped to transform the face of Rome in the Catholic resurgence of the 17th century. It is the seat of one of the most important Counter-Reformatory movements, St Phillip Neri's Oratorians. St Phillip originally wanted the nave simply whitewashed, but did not reckon on the exuberant baroque fresco cycles that were to make their dazzling mark in Roman churches half a century later. The breath-taking example here is Pietro da Cortona's (on the nave ceiling, dome and apse, 1647–56). Next door is Borromini's superb Oratory façade (1637–40), which is cunningly detailed.

🕂 5F 📧 Piazza della Chiesa Nuova 🕐 Daily 7–12, 4–7 🚍 40, 46, 62, 64 to Piazza della Chiesa Nuova

COLONNA DI MARCO AURELIO

In the square outside Palazzo Chigi, the prime minister's official residence and the offices of the newspaper *Il Tempo,* is an intricately carved column erected in memory of Emperor Marcus Aurelius after his death in AD180. It is about 30m (98ft) high and depicts scenes from the Emperor's successful German campaign. The statue of St Paul at the top of the column replaced the original of Marcus Aurelius on the orders of Pope Sixtus V in 1588.

✚ 8E ✉ Piazza Colonna
🚌 62, 63, 85, 95, 117, 119 and services to Via del Corso

FONTANA DELLE TARTARUGHE

This delightfully delicate fountain, in Piazza Mattei, showing four male nymphs with tantalizingly enigmatic smiles cavorting provocatively around its edges, was the work of Giacomo della Porta and Taddeo Landini in the 1580s. The contrastingly precarious tortoises are believed to have been added by Bernini in the following century. According to legend, the fountain was erected overnight by the Duke of Mattei, who wanted to show his potential father-in-law that he was still capable of achieving great things even though he had just lost his fortune. He also had one of the windows of his palace blocked up so that nobody else would ever see the fountain from that superb vantage point.

✚ 16H ✉ Piazza Mattei 🚌 30, 70, 87, 116 to Largo di Torre Argentina

IL GESÙ

This church spans the whole of the baroque: from the floor plan (by Vignola, 1568, and probably based on the ideas of one of Michelangelo's last architectural plans), through the façade (with its triangular pediment and side scrolls) and dome (by Giacomo della Porta, 1575) to Pietro da Cortona's altar of St Xavier (1674) and Andrea Pozzo's almost vulgarly ornate chapel of St Ignatius (1696). This is the central church of the Jesuits, the severe order founded by Ignatius Loyola in the 16th century – its design has been imitated in Jesuit church-building all over the world. Next door are the rooms occupied by Loyola (usually open when the church is), which have a wonderful *trompe l'oeil* fresco by Pozzo.

🜨 17G ✉ Piazza del Gesù
☎ 06 6970 0232 🕐 Daily
6–12:30, 4–7:15 🚌 40, 46, 62, 63, 64, 70 and services to Largo di Torre Argentina

THE GHETTO

The Jewish community in Rome is one of the
oldest in Europe and dates from the first
century BC, although it first settled this area
north of Isola Tiberina (➤ 108) in the 13th
century. From the mid-16th century until
Italian Unification in 1870 Roman Jews were
enclosed behind high walls in this warren of
narrow, winding alleyways, which still house kosher butchers,
excellent Jewish restaurants and a baker offering Roman-Jewish
specials such as *torta di ricotta* and sweet 'pizzas' made with
candied and dried fruit. At the heart of the ghetto was the old fish
market, held in front of the Portico d'Ottavia, the only remains of a
vast shop and temple complex, renovated in the first century BC
and named after Emperor Augustus's sister Octavia.

✚ 16H ✉ Via del Portico d'Ottavia (and the streets north) 🚌 H, 8, 63, 630,
780 to Via Arenula

GIANICOLO

The hill that rises
between Trastevere
and the Vatican to the
southwest of the

Tiber has some of the
best views of central
Rome and is a
popular lovers' tryst.
At its summit is
Piazza Giuseppe
Garibaldi, where a rousing equestrian statue of Giuseppe Garibaldi
commemorates his 1849 victory over the French here, when
he led the troops of the Roman Republic in the struggle for
Italian unification.

✚ 13H ✉ Passeggiata del Gianicolo 🚌 870 to Passeggiata del Gianicolo

ISOLA TIBERINA

From the right-hand (Ghetto-) side of the river, Isola Tiberina is reached via the oldest original bridge over the Tiber, the Ponte Fabricio (62BC). Originally the walls of the buildings rose directly out of the river, but since the end of the 19th century the island has been surrounded by a wide embankment, now a popular spot for enjoying early-season sun. The church of San Bartolomeo was built in the 10th century on the site of a third-century BC temple to the god of healing, Aesculapius, and the connection with health has been continued by the Fatebenefratelli hospital, which now covers most of the island. Downstream you can see the one remaining arch of the Ponte Rotto (broken bridge), which was the

first stone bridge in Rome (142BC), although it had already fallen down at least twice before this mid-16th-century rebuild collapsed in 1598.

✚ 16J ✉ Isola Tiberina 🚌 H, 23, 63, 280 to Lungotevere dei Cenci or to Lungotevere Anguillara

LARGO DI TORRE ARGENTINA

Behind one of the busiest bus intersections in the Area Sacra at Largo di Torre Argentina are the remains of four Republican-era temples, known as temples A, B, C and D (in alphabetical order, starting nearest the main bus stop). Temple C is the oldest (fourth century BC) while third-century BC Temple A was used as a church during the Middle Ages (there are the remains of two apses). Behind it are the drains of a massive public toilet. Julius Caesar was murdered near here in 44BC, when the Senate was using the Curia of Pompey as a meeting place while the main senate house was being restored. The area is rarely open to the public.

✚ 16G ✉ Largo di Torre Argentina ⏲ Some evenings in summer for guided tours in English and Italian 🚌 40, 46, 62, 63, 64, 70, 81, 492, 628, 780, 916 to Largo di Torre Argentina

MUSEO BARRACCO

This is one of Rome's most charming museums, but is often overlooked. The exquisite, small collection of Assyrian, Egyptian, Greek and Roman sculptures (including a series of Roman heads minus their noses) and artefacts was created by Senator Giovanni Barracco and presented to the city in 1902. Underneath the museum (ask the attendants to take you down) are remains of what is said to be a Roman fish shop, complete with counter and a water trough. Fresco fragments (from the fourth century AD) found there are displayed on the ground floor.

www.comune.roma.it/museobarracco

✚ 15G ✉ Corso Vittorio Emanuele II 168 ☎ 06 6880 6848 ⏲ Temporarily closed for restoration; check with tourist office

Gianicolo to the Ghetto

Start at Piazzale G Garibaldi, on the Gianicolo (► 107), where there are some great views.

Follow the road southeast, past the busts of heroes of the Risorgimento, to the gateway; turn left down the staircase.

But first look at the monumental baroque Fontana Paola, where people once washed their clothes.

Follow the road down past the Spanish Embassy and turn left on Via Garibaldi. Go to the bottom where, left, is Porta Settimiana (1498), the gateway pilgrims used to reach the Vatican. Turn right down Via della Scala.

The church of Santa Maria della Scala dates from the late 16th century. Its plain façade hides a rich, cluttered interior.

Continue into Piazza San Egidio, past the Museo di Roma in Trastevere (▶ 112), and go left, passing Vicolo del Piede into Piazza Santa Maria in Trastevere.

Admire the church (▶ 125), with its 12th-century mosaics on the façade, and the fountain by Carlo Fontana (1692).

Continue straight through the piazza and follow Via della Lungaretta to Piazza Sidney Sonnino.

On the right is the 12th-century belltower of the ancient church of San Crisogono, rebuilt in the 16th century.

Cross the piazza. The left-corner tower is 13th-century and home to the Dante Society. Go on to Piazza di Piscinula, turn left up a staircase along the side of an old palace and cross the Lungotevere to get to Isola Tiberina (▶ 108).

Isola Tiberina somewhat resembles a ship and was a strategic point in ancient times, being one of the few points at which the Tiber could be easily crossed.

Cross the island to the Ghetto (▶ 107); on the right is the Synagogue (1874). Straight ahead, the Via Portico d'Ottavia has a choice of cafés and restaurants.

Distance 4km (2.5 miles)
Time 2 hours without stops, or 4 with stops for coffee and visits
Start point Piazzale G Garibaldi ✚ 13H 🚌 41
End point The Ghetto ✚ 16H 🚌 44
Lunch La Taverna del Ghetto (€)
✉ Via Portico d'Ottavia 8 ☎ 06 6880 9771

MUSEO DI ROMA IN TRASTEVERE

The museum opened in 1978 in a former Carmelite convent behind the church of Santa Maria in Trastevere (➤ 125). Everyday life in 17th- and 18th-century Italy, including festivals and customs, is illustrated by various paintings, prints, reconstructions and waxworks, all among an interesting diversity of objects from the period when the popes ruled Rome. There is also memorabilia relating to famous Roman poets, including Giuseppe Gioacchino Belli and Carlo Alberto Salustri (better known as Trilussa). Each of these local-dialect poets has a Trastevere square named after him.

www.comune.roma.it/museodiroma.trastevere

➕ 15J ✉ Piazza Sant'Egidio 1/b ☎ 06 581 6563 🕔 Tue–Sun 10–8 🚌 23, 280 to Lungotevere Sanzio ♿ Moderate

PALAZZO CORSINI

This palace was once the residence of Queen Christina of Sweden, who sought refuge in the city after converting to Roman Catholicism in the 17th century. It now houses part of the national art collection (the more important part is at Palazzo Barberini, ➤ 48–49). The galleries, decorated with arresting trompe l'oeil frescoes, are filled predominantly with paintings from the 16th and 17th centuries. In room 1 Van Dyck's superb Madonna della Paglia and Murillo's Madonna and Child stand out among many other paintings of the same subject; one by Girolamo Siciolante de Sermoneta is frightening in its awfulness, with an over-rosy, muscular baby seeming to choke on its mother's milk. Do not miss the paintings of the Bologna school in room 7, among which Guido Reni's vibrant and expressive St Jerome and melancholy Salome, Giovanni Lanfranco's very beautiful St Peter Healing St Agatha and the haunting Ecce Homo by Guercino are highlights.

➕ 14H ✉ Via della Lungara 10 ☎ 06 6880 2323; book online at www.ticketeria.it or call 06 328 101 🕔 Tue–Sat 8:30–1:30, Sun 8:30–7 ♿ Moderate 🚌 23, 116, 280, 870 to Lungotevere della Farnesina

PALAZZO DORIA PAMPHILJ

The seat of the noble Roman family since the late Renaissance, Palazzo Doria Pamphilj takes up an entire block of Via del Corso. In the grand reception rooms and the original picture galleries the paintings are hung exactly as they were in the 18th century, cluttered side by side from floor to ceiling. Four rooms house masterpieces from the 15th to 17th centuries, including works by Hans Memling, Raphael, Titian, Tintoretto and two early paintings by Caravaggio. The star of the collection is the Velasquez portrait of Pope Innocent X, majestically positioned in its own chamber. For an extra charge, take a guided tour of the fascinating private apartments (currently closed for restoration).

www.doriapamphilj.it

➕ 17G ✉ Piazza del Collegio Romano 2 ☎ 06 679 7323; book online at www.ticketeria.it ⏱ Apartments: guided tours only, 10:30–12:30. Gallery: Fri–Wed 10–5 ✋ Expensive 🚌 62, 63, 81, 85, 95, 117, 119 and services to Via del Corso; 44, 46, 84, 715, 716, 780, 781, 810, 916 to Piazza Venezia

PALAZZO MADAMA

This pretty little palace has been the seat of the Italian senate since 1871, hence the armed police and military guard. It was built as the Medici family's Roman residence in the 16th century, although the Madame after whom it was named was Margaret of Parma, an illegitimate daughter of Emperor Charles V who lived here in the 1560s. The icing-like stucco façade was added in the 17th century.

www.senato.it

✚ 7F ✉ Piazza Madama 11

☎ 06 67061 ⏱ First Sat in each month 10–6; guided visits in Italian only

✋ Free 🚌 30, 70, 81, 87, 116, 492, 628 to Corso del Rinascimento

PALAZZO DI MONTECITORIO

Bernini did the original designs for this concave palace, although all that remains of his work are the clock tower, the columns and the window sills. In 1871 it became the Chamber of Deputies, and had doubled in size by 1918. In the piazza in front of the palace there are often political demonstrations; a strong police presence keeps people at a respectful distance from the entrance, used by Italy's 630 parliamentarians. The obelisk in the piazza was brought from Egypt by Augustus in 10BC to act as the pointer of a giant (but inaccurate) sundial in Campo Marzio. It was moved here in 1787.

www.camera.it

✚ 7E ✉ Piazza di Montecitorio ☎ 06 67061 ⏱ First Sun in each month 10–6; guided tours in Italian only 🚌 62, 63 and all services to Via del Corso

PALAZZO SPADA

Built in 1540, this palace was acquired by Cardinal Bernardino Spada in the 17th century. In addition to housing his collection in the Galleria Spada, the palace is the seat of the Italian Council of State and thus under prominent *Carabinieri* guard. Among the 17th- and 18th-century paintings are a jewel-like *Visitation,* attributed to Andrea del Sarto, and works by Guercino and Rubens. Cardinal Spada also collected Roman sculpture – the restored *Seated Philosopher* is a highlight.

The most delightful aspect of the palace is Borromini's ingenious *trompe l'oeil* perspective in the lower courtyard (you will need to ask the attendants or porter to let you in). A long colonnade stretches out to a large statue at the end. Go closer to see that the colonnade is in fact only a quarter of the length it seems, and that the statue is much smaller than it first appears.

🕂 15H ✉ Piazza Capo di Ferro 13 ☎ 06 687 4893; book online at www.ticketeria.it 🕙 Tue–Sat 8:30–7:30, Sun 9–6:30 ✋ Moderate 🚌 280 to Lungotevere dei Tebaldi; H, 8, 63, 680, 780 to Via Arenula

PALAZZO VENEZIA

Rome's most important collection of medieval decorative arts includes fine examples of Byzantine jewellery, silver work, ceramics, porcelain, tapestries and armour. There is a superb group of intricately carved Florentine wooden marriage chests, some small 16th-century bronzes and fine religious paintings by early Renaissance artists. Palazzo Venezia often hosts special exhibitions in the opulent main halls overlooking the piazza. Mussolini used the vast Sala del Mappamondo as an office and used the balcony to address the crowds below.

🞤 17G 🖂 Via del Plebiscito 118 ☎ 06 6999 4318; online bookings www.ticketeria.it 🕐 Tue–Sun 8:30–7; times may vary 🖐 Moderate 🚌 44, 46, 84, 715, 716, 780, 781, 810, 916 to Piazza Venezia

PANTHEON

Best places to see, ➤ 50–51.

PASQUINO

Physically, Pasquino has seen better days; all that remains of this third-century BC sculpture near Piazza Navona is a twisted torso and a weather-beaten face. But for several centuries after he was propped up here in the early 16th century Pasquino played an important role as Rome's most talkative 'talking statue'. During the days of papal rule (until 1870) there were few safe outlets for dissent and those with political or social axes to grind came at dead of night to attach their written complaints to one of the talking statues.

🞤 6F 🖂 Piazza di Pasquino 🚌 46, 64 and services to Corso Vittorio Emanuele II

PIAZZA FARNESE

Dominated by Palazzo Farnese, which was designed for Farnese Pope Paulo III in the 1530s by – among others – Michelangelo, this spacious, nearly traffic-free square is a peaceful contrast to the buzz of nearby Campo de'Fiori (➤ 102) and a good spot for a quiet rest. The palace is now the French Embassy and at night Caracci's ceiling paintings on the first floor are illuminated. The two vast granite fountains were assembled in the 17th century from bathtubs found at Caracalla's baths (➤ 94–95). They are decorated with lilies, the Farnese family crest.

✚ 15H ✉ Piazza Farnese 🚌 46, 62, 64 and all to Corso Vittorio Emanuele II

PIAZZA NAVONA

Best places to see, ➤ 52–53.

PONTE SANT'ANGELO

This is certainly the most elegant of the bridges over the Tiber. Bernini designed the ten angels that adorn its balustrades, each displaying one of the devices of Christ's passion, in 1667. Their ecstatically swooning expressions earned them the nickname of the 'Breezy Maniacs'. Two more angels, deemed too beautiful to withstand the rigours of the Roman climate, are on display in the church of Sant'Andrea delle Fratte in Via di Sant'Andrea delle Fratte. Most of the bridge dates from the 17th and 19th centuries but the central arches are the remains of the bridge that Emperor Hadrian built here in the second century AD to lead to his tomb (now the Castel Sant'Angelo, ➤ 40–41).

✚ 5E ✉ Ponte Sant'Angelo 🚌 40, 62 to Lungotevere Castello; 30, 34, 49, 87, 926, 990 and services to Piazza Cavour

SANT'AGOSTINO

This important early Renaissance church contains a sculpture of the pregnant Mary by Sansovino (1518–21), an altar with Bernini angels and a Byzantine Madonna. The main attractions are, however, the paintings by Raphael and Guercino and Caravaggio's beautiful *Madonna di Loreto* (painted in 1606, just before he had to flee Rome to escape a murder charge). Caravaggio's realistic portayal of biblical figures as poor people, usually (as here) illuminated in the foreground and forming a strong diagonal across the picture, were criticized for lack of decorum because of their dirty feet, ripped clothes and perhaps too-human Madonna.

Sant'Agostino was where many of Rome's most sought-after courtesans came to worship, attracting a large following of male admirers. For an attractive, go-getting Renaissance girl, life as the kept woman of a Roman aristocrat (or even a senior church man; many of the popes' so-called nephews were really their sons) could lead to riches and a successful career (like the mother of Lucrezia and Cesare Borgia, who bought and ran three hotels).

✚ 6E ✉ Piazza S. Agostino ☎ 06 880 1962 ⏱ Daily 8–12, 4:30–7:30
🚌 30, 70, 81, 87, 116 to Corso del Rinascimento

SANT'ANDREA DELLA VALLE

Another great Counter-Reformatory church to put Protestantism on the defensive and accommodate yet another new Order (the Theatines, founded in 1524). Designed by Della Porta (1591), it has a superb and imposing travertine façade (Rainaldi, 1655–63) and Carlo Maderno's impressive dome (1622), which is second only to that of St Peter's and also contains one of the church's important baroque fresco cycles. Other frescoes, by competitors Lanfranco and Domenichino in the dome and Domenichino's *Scenes from the Life and Death of St Andrew* in the apse, have been restored. Opera fans note that this is where the opening scene of Puccini's *Tosca* takes place.

✚ 16G ✉ Corso Vittorio Emanuele II ☎ 06 686 1339 ⏱ Daily 7:30–12:30, 4:30–7:30 🚌 46, 64 and services to Corso Vittorio Emanuele II; 30, 70, 81, 87, 116, 492, 628 to Corso del Rinascimento

SANTA CECILIA IN TRASTEVERE

Approached through a delightful courtyard, this church contains one of the most beautiful baroque sculptures in Rome (by Stefano Maderno, 1599), showing a tiny St Cecilia, the patron saint of music. Supposedly in the position of her nasty death (it took her three days to die but she sang throughout), her head is poignantly turns from our gaze. You will also find frescoes by Cavallini of the *Last Judgement* (1293), painted in beautifully soft powdery blues, greens and pinks. Underneath the church, the remains of a Roman house and shops, including a mosaic, can still be seen.

✚ 16J ✉ Piazza Santa Cecilia in Trastevere 22 ☎ 06 589 9289 ⏱ Daily 9:30–12:30, 4–6:30. Cavallini frescoes: Mon–Sat 10:15–12:15, Sun 11–12:30 ✋ Church free; excavations and frescoes inexpensive 🚌 56, 60, 75, 710, 780 to Viale Trastevere

SAN FRANCESCO A RIPA

A 13th-century monastery was built on the site of an inn where St Francis of Assisi supposedly stayed, but the present church is baroque (1692, by de'Rossi, working under Bernini). Architecturally uninteresting, it does, however, house one of Bernini's most splendid works (*The Blessed Ludovica Albertoni*, 1674). Framed in the last left chapel, she is best approached head-on from the nave. Depicted in feverish death throes after her life of good works, the agonized writhings of the deeply cut white folds of her clothes create a powerful impact. The textures of hair, skin or the bed are not differentiated and the whiteness is intensified by the dark foreground drapes, close enough to touch.

✚ 16K ✉ Piazza San Francesco d'Assisi ☎ 06 588 1331 ◷ Daily 7–12, 4–7 🚌 23, 280, 630, 780 to Largo di Torre Argentina, then tram 8 to Viale Trastevere

SANT'IGNAZIO DI LOYOLA

This is Rome's second Jesuit church – the first being Il Gesù, ➤ 106. The interior is a late-baroque (1626–50) assault on the senses, epitomized by Jesuit artist Andrea Pozzo's astonishing fresco in the nave – *Apotheosis of St Ignatius* (1691). An extraordinary feat of perspective, the *trompe l'oeil* architecture becomes indistinguishable from the real. The dome, too, is painted (find the spot, move and watch the perspective distort). Similarly sumptuous are St Aloysius' tomb, with its lapis lazuli urn, and the altar with Legros' relief sculpture (right transept 1698–99). The friezes are by one of the baroque period's finest, Algardi.

✚ 8F ✉ Piazza di Sant'Ignazio ☎ 06 679 4406 ◷ Daily 7:30–12:30, 3–7:15 🚌 62, 81, 492, 628 to Via del Corso; 116 to Largo di Torre Argentina

SANT'IVO ALLA SAPIENZA

Not far from the Pantheon in Piazza Sant'
Eustachio is the domed church of Sant'Ivo alla
Sapienza, one of Borromini's masterpieces.
Built in the grounds of the Palazzo alla Sapienza,
the University of Rome until 1935, the church is
worth visiting for its extraordinary spiralling
dome surmounted by a crown of flames.
Entrance to the church is through the cloister.

🕂 7F ✉ Corso del Rinascimento, 40 ☎ 06 686 4987
🕓 Mon–Fri 8:30–5, Sat, Sun 9–12 🚌 30, 70, 81, 87,
116, 492, 628 and services to Corso del Rinascimento

SAN LUIGI DEI FRANCESI

Founded in 1518 by Cardinal Giulio de' Medici
(later Pope Clement VII) this, the French national
church, is worth visiting mainly for its paintings,
including a *St Cecilia* by Domenichino (1616)
and Reni. The *pièces de résistance* are,
however, the works by Caravaggio: *The Calling
of St Matthew* and *The Martyrdom of St
Matthew* (1599), in the Contarelli chapel. Both
exemplify the artist's use of artificial lighting,
which casts the backgrounds into deep
darkness, focuses attention on the story's
essential elements and moulds the remarkably
everyday figures who dominate the foreground.
This everyday quality was perceived as
irreverent and the most notorious example,
St Matthew and the Angel (1602), is above the
altar (note the dirty feet).

🕂 6F ✉ Piazza San Luigi dei Francesci 5 ☎ 06 688 271
🕓 Daily 8:30–12:30, 3:30–7 (closed Thu pm) 🚌 30, 70,
81, 87, 116, 492, 628 to Corso del Rinascimento

SANTA MARIA SOPRA MINERVA

Bernini's engaging obelisk-bearing baby elephant (1667) sits in the piazza in front of this eclectic church (built in 1280, completed in 1500, modified in the 17th century). Inside, there is many a fine work: Bernini's wind-blown marble monument to Maria Raggi (1643) and another to GB Vigevano (1617); Michelangelo's *Redeemer with his Cross* (1520); and the rich and lavish Aldobrandini chapel (della Porta and C Maderna, 1600–5), once again bearing witness to important Roman families making

their own mark on baroque Rome. The treats, however, are Renaissance, notably the stunning frescoes by Lippi. St Valentine was made the patron saint of lovers here in 1465.

✚ 7F ✉ Piazza della Minerva 42 ☎ 06 679 3926 🄰 Mon–Sat 7–7, Sun 8–7 (10–6 in winter) 🚍 30, 40, 46, 62, 64, 70, 81, 87 and services to Largo di Torre Argentina

SANTA MARIA IN TRASTEVERE

The 12th-century mosaics on the façade of this church create a magical backdrop to the piazza, the heart of this characteristic quarter. Inside the basilica (third and fourth centuries, rebuilt in the 12th) is the glorious expanse of gold of the apse mosaic. This is the oldest church in Rome dedicated to Mary, and she is represented with almost equal stature to Christ in the mosaic's upper panel (c1140), below a fan-like kaleidoscopic design of luxuriant blue. In the panels below are a series of exquisitely delicate representations of her life by Pietro Cavallini, who was working in the late 13th century. There is also a cosmati floor and a ceiling by Domenichino, designed in 1617.

✚ 15J ✉ Piazza Santa Maria in Trastevere ☎ 06 581 9443 🄰 Daily 7:45am–8/9pm (may close 12:30–3:30) 🚍 8, 630, 780, H to Viale Trastevere

SAN PIETRO IN MONTORIO

Here you'll find Bernini's Raimondi chapel, a key precursor to the Cornaro Chapel (▶ 149, Santa Maria della Vittoria) for its lighting effects. More significant is Bramante's *tempietto* (little temple) in the courtyard of the adjoining monastery (1502), a seminal work in the history of architecture. Its perfectly proportioned simplicity and dignity, in keeping with the commemoration of the (alleged) spot of Peter's crucifixion, expresses the Renaissance ideal of emulating classical architecture.

✚ 14J ✉ Piazza San Pietro in Montorio 2 ☎ 06 581 3940 🄰 Church: daily 9–12, 4–6. *Tempietto:* Tue–Sun 9:30–12:30, 4–6 (2–4 Nov–Apr) 🚍 870 to Gianicolo

TEATRO DI MARCELLO

Here 2,000 years of Roman history can be seen at a glance. The lower part of the multi-levelled and many-styled building comprises the surviving two levels of a three-storey theatre that Julius Caesar started. Augustus finished the theatre in the first century BC and named it after one of his nephews. The elegant 16th-century palace, dramatically built on top of these crumbling remains (which served as, among other uses, a medieval fortress) and now divided into luxury apartments, was built by Baldassarre Peruzzi. The strange, reddish protuberance stuck on the southern end is a 1930s Fascist addition, supposedly in keeping with the style of the theatre. To the north are three delicate Corinthian columns, part of a Temple of Apollo which was rebuilt in the first century BC. In summer, classical music concerts are held outside.

✚ 17H ✉ Via del Teatro di Marcello ☎ 06 5752 5041 🚌 30, 44, 95, 170, 716, 781 to Via del Teatro di Marcello ❓ Tours are available

TEMPI DI VESTA E DELLA FORTUNA VIRILIS

Neither of these photogenic, small but perfectly formed temples have anything to do with Vesta or *Fortuna Virilis* (manly fortune). The round one, which dates from the first century BC and is the same shape as the temple of Vesta in the Forum

(➤ 44–45), was dedicated to Hercules. The rectangular one, dating from the second century BC, was probably dedicated to Portunus, the god of ports; this was the port area of ancient Rome. Across the piazza is the fourth-century double arch of Janus, named after the two-headed guardian of the underworld.

✚ 17J ✉ Piazza della Bocca della Verità 🚌 160, 628, 715 to Piazza della Bocca della Verità

VILLA FARNESINA

Baldassare Peruzzi built this delicate little villa in 1508 for the rich banker Agostino Chigi, who was also a patron of Raphael. Now it is used for temporary exhibitions, although its otherwise empty rooms are also worth visiting for their spectacular frescoes by Raphael, whose *Triumph of Galatea* is on the ground floor, along with the *Loggia di Psiche,* which he designed. Sodoma's seductive fresco of the *Marriage of Alexander the Great and Roxanne* is painted against a *trompe l'oeil* background of views of contemporary Rome.

www.lincei.it/informazioni

✚ 14H ✉ Via della Lungara 230 ☎ 06 6802 7268 🕐 Mon–Sat 9–1 ✋ Moderate 🚌 23, 280 to Lungotevere della Farnesina

HOTELS

Campo de'Fiori (€€)

Situated in one of the loveliest quarters of central Rome, this hotel has a terrace overlooking Roman rooftops and is in a flaking ochre-hued street. The décor is pleasant and there are multi-lingual staff.

✉ Via del Biscione 6 ☎ 06 688 06865; www.hotelcampde fiori.com 🚌 To Corso Vittorio Emanuele II, Largo di Torre Argentina

In Parione Piccolo (€€)

In a great location close to Campo de'Fiori, with a rooftop garden.

✉ Via Chiavari 32 ☎ 06 6880 2560; www.inparione.com 🚌 To Corso Vittorio Emanuele II

Navona (€)

For a one-star hotel, Navona is a find. Only one minute from the Piazza Navona and most of the 15 rooms have been renovated to a good standard. It's best to take breakfast at a nearby bar.

✉ Via dei Sediari 8 ☎ 06 686 4203; www.hotelnavona.com
🚌 To Corso del Rinascimento

Portoghesi (€€)

Tucked away in a lovely side street in one of Rome's prettiest areas, Portoghesi is tastefully furnished, with a roof terrace.

✉ Via dei Portoghesi 1 ☎ 06 686 4231; www.hotelportoghesiroma.com
🚌 To Corso del Rinascimento

Ripa (€€€)

Space and light are optimized at this Trastevere hotel, decorated in a minimalist style and popular with visiting Italians. There is a restaurant.

✉ Via Luigi Gianniti 21 ☎ 06 5833 3583; www.ripahotel.com 🚌 To Viale Trastevere

Smeraldo (€€)

In an excellent location, just a short walk from the Campo de'Fiori.

✉ Vicolo dei Chiodaroli 9 ☎ 06 687 5929; www.smeraldoroma.com
🚌 To Corso Vittorio Emanuele II, Largo di Torre Argentina

RESTAURANTS

Augusto (€)

This historic Roman trattoria has characteristic paper-covered tables (outside in summer). Happy confusion reigns here and service may be slapdash but the Roman cooking is genuine. Go early to enjoy the best dishes.

✉ Piazza de' Renzi 15 ☎ 06 580 3798 🕐 Daily 🚌 To Piazza Sidney Sonnino

Il Bacaro (€€)

A candle-lit romantic restaurant especially popular with young people both for its atmosphere and its location (near the Pantheon). Outside tables in summer. Innovative Italian dishes, affable service and an extensive wine list.

✉ Via degli Spagnoli 27 ☎ 06 686 4110 🕐 Mon–Sat 🚌 To Largo di Torre Argentina

Da Baffetto (€)

Immensely popular central pizzeria, with a crowd often jostling to get past the door. Service is swift and efficient, and the pizzas are worth the wait. Not a place for lingering. Open late.

✉ Via del Governo Vecchio 114 ☎ 06 686 1617 🕐 Daily dinner only
🚌 To Corso Vittorio Emanuele II

Ciak (€€)

A rustic Tuscan bistro for lovers of game, roast meats and inimitable local dishes. Friendly seating arrangements and an open grill add to the enjoyment.

✉ Vicolo del Cinque 21 ☎ 06 589 4774 🕐 Mon–Fri dinner only, Sat–Sun lunch and dinner 🚌 To Piazza Sonnino

Il Convivio (€€€)

A prime choice for a special occasion: creative cuisine is spiced with a touch of genius and true professionalism. Both the well-balanced set menus and the *à la carte* dishes are tantalizing in their range and variety and there's a comparable wine list.

✉ Vicolo dei Soldati 31 ☎ 06 686 9432 🕐 Mon–Sat dinner only
🚌 To Corso del Rinascimento

Ditirambo (€€)

The two beamed rooms with tiled floors have the tranquillity of an old country inn; innovative Italian dishes are based on genuine ingredients and subtle combinations. Homemade bread, pasta and desserts; excellent (house) wine. Informative staff.

✉ Piazza della Cancelleria 74 ☎ 06 687 1626 🕓 Tue–Sun lunch and dinner, Mon dinner only 🚌 To Corso Vittorio Emanuele II

Enoteca Corsi (€)

An old-fashioned and comfortable spot for a simple lunch. Genuine Roman food, informal service and friendly diners eager to share their table space. The adjoining wine shop is also recommended.

✉ Via del Gesù 87/88 ☎ 06 679 0821 🕓 Mon–Sat lunch only 🚌 To Largo di Torre Argentina

Grappolo d'Oro (€)

A stone's throw from Campo de' Fiori, this pleasant trattoria offers basic Roman fare at prices that are more than reasonable for such a location. Discreet, cordial service.

✉ Piazza della Cancelleria 80 ☎ 06 689 7080 🕓 Daily, may close for lunch Tue–Fri in winter 🚌 To Corso Vittorio Emanuele II

Ivo a Trastevere (€)

Go early to avoid the evening queue, as this is the best known of Trastevere's pizzerias. Enjoy a classic Roman pizza and join the scores of contented customers who can say that they have eaten here. Air quality may make the tables outside less pleasant.

✉ Via San Francesco a Ripa 158 ☎ 06 581 7082 🕓 Wed–Mon dinner only 🚌 To Piazza Sidney Sonnino, Viale Trastevere

Da Lucia (€)

Catch the last glimpses of the fading glories of one of Trastevere's culinary historic spots. Genuine Roman dishes are traditionally and carefully prepared and served without undue ceremony, as is the wine. Sit outside in summer and take in the local atmosphere.

✉ Vicolo del Mattonato 2b ☎ 06 580 3601 🕓 Tue–Sun 🚌 To Piazza Sidney Sonnino

Navona Notte (€)

Popular with locals for many years and known for its excellent pasta and some of the largest and tastiest pizzas in Rome, this place offers excellent value for money and is in a good position near Piazza Navona. Check out the Tempieto della Pace church around the corner, superbly lit at night.

✉ Via del Teatro Pace 44 ☎ 06 686 9278 🕓 Mon–Sat dinner only, Sun lunch and dinner 🚌 To Corso Vittorio Emanuele II

Panattoni (€)

A hugely popular Trastevere pizzeria nicknamed 'the coffin-maker' (cassamortaro) for its characteristic marble-topped tables. Watch the chef's flamboyant flipping of pizzas at the large oven inside or scramble for an outside table in summer.

✉ Viale Trastevere 53 ☎ 06 580 0919 🕓 Thu–Tue dinner only
🚌 To Viale Trastevere

Da Paris (€€)

Satisfied customers who return again and again to this elegant restaurant attest to the winning formula of Trastevere's prime Roman-Jewish restaurant: unchanging traditional dishes and the use of fresh ingredients. Highlights include delicate vegetable *fritto misto* and delicious fresh fish. There's a small terrace in front and lofty rooms within. The wine list is well selected.

✉ Piazza San Calisto 7a ☎ 06 581 5378 🕓 Tue–Sat lunch and dinner, Sun lunch only 🚌 To Viale Trastevere

Piperno (€€€)

At the heart of the Jewish Ghetto, the name Piperno has been synonymous with the best (and not inexpensive) Roman-Jewish cuisine for more than 100 years. Time really does seem to stand still in this restaurant: the old-fashioned interior is a sombre backdrop, the waiters exude an olde-worlde chivalry and the classic food is consistently genuine. Reserve ahead.

✉ Via Monte de' Cenci 9 ☎ 06 6880 2772 🕓 Tue–Sat lunch and dinner, Sun lunch only 🚌 To Via Arenula

Ponziani (€€)

Set in a scenic quiet piazza of Trastevere, and particularly atmospheric in summer, this elegant little restaurant (aptly named after culinary over-indulgence) specializes in Mediterranean and Calabrian fish dishes. Various reasonable set menus. Friendly, attentive service.

✉ Piazza de' Ponziani 7a ☎ 06 581 4529 🕓 Tue–Sun 🚌 To Viale Trastevere

Roma Sparita (€)

Located in a medieval square in Trastevere and dominated by the church of St Cecilia, this restaurant serves genuine Roman cuisine, with dishes such as beef strips with porcini mushrooms. Try the risotto with radicchio and walnuts. Pizzas are baked traditionally in a wood-burning oven and there are excellent homemade desserts. Wash it down with wine from the Castelli Romana. Outside dining in summer.

✉ Piazza S Cecilia 24 ☎ 06 580 0757 🕓 Tue–Sat lunch and dinner, Sun lunch only 🚌 To Viale di Trastevere

La Rosetta (€€€)

One of Rome's most famous fish restaurants is located near the Pantheon. Dishes are simply prepared – but with flair and creativity – to retain the best taste, using only the freshest ingredients. Try the lobster with herbs and cheese or red prawns with Sauterne and sage. There's an excellent wine list and it's the place to dress up and experience elegant dining. La Rosetta is popular, so reserve ahead.

✉ Via della Rosetta 8–9 ☎ 06 686 1002 🕓 Mon–Sat 🚌 Piazza della Rotunda or Corso del Rinascimento

Sora Lella (€€)

A legendary Roman institution on the enchanting Tiber Island. The food is, naturally, Roman; the diners may be illustrious. Service is charming and informative.

✉ Via del Ponte Quattro Capi 16 ☎ 06 686 1601 🕓 Mon–Sat. Closed Aug 🚌 To Lungotevere de' Cenci, Lungotevere Anguillare

SHOPPING

ANTIQUES
La Sinopia
You'll find objects of high quality in this store, on a street with several antiques shops.

✉ Via dei Banchi Nuovi 21a/21c ☎ 06 687 2869 🚌 To Corso Vittorio Emanuele II

ART
Maria Grazia Luffarelli
Specializes in watercolours, especially land and seascapes. Also a range of Roman watercolour reproductions in postcard form.

✉ Via dei Banchi Vecchi 29 ☎ 06 683 2494 🚌 To Corso Vittorio Emanuele II

BOOKS
Feltrinelli
The best-stocked bookshop chain in Rome.

✉ Largo di Torre Argentina 5a ☎ 06 6880 3248 🚌 To Largo di Torre Argentina

CHILDREN'S CLOTHES AND TOYS
Città del Sole
An inspired selection of top-of-the-range educational toys and books for children of all ages.

✉ Via della Scrofa 65 ☎ 06 6880 3805 🚌 To Corso del Rinascimento

FASHION
Arsenale
Located just off Piazza Navona, owner Patrizia Pieroni's outlet showcases her own romantic designs.

✉ Via del Governo Vecchio 64 ☎ 06 686 1380 🚌 To Corso Vittorio Emanuele II

Davide Cenci
High quality, classic and classy, Davide Cenci is synonymous in Rome with low-key tailored elegance.

✉ Via Campo Marzio 1/7 ☎ 06 699 0681 🚌 To Largo di Torre Argentina

HATS
Borsalino
An old-fashioned hat shop that is the most famous in Rome for its classic men's headwear and more changeable women's styles.

✉ Piazza del Popolo 20 ☎ 06 323 3353 🚇 Flaminio 🚌 To Piazza Popolo

MARKETS
Campo de' Fiori
Probably the loveliest food market in central Rome thanks to the wonderful piazza hosting it. Open every morning except Sundays.

✉ Piazza Campo de' Fiori 🚌 To Corso Vittorio Emanuele II

Porta Portese
This market is famous throughout Italy. It takes over the streets in and around Porta Portese every Sunday morning and is jam-packed. You can buy almost everything imaginable from clothes (beware of fake labels) to books and antiques.

✉ Via Porta Portese 🚌 To Viale Trastevere

STATIONERY
Pantheon
A gorgeous little shop that sells hand-marbled paper, notebooks and photo albums, as well as writing paper and cards.

✉ Via della Rotonda 15 ☎ 06 687 5313 🚌 To Largo di Torre Argentina

ENTERTAINMENT

NIGHTLIFE
Cul de Sac
A small and long-established wine bar close to Piazza Navona, with more than 1,400 wines, plus snacks and light meals.

✉ Piazza Pasquino 73 ☎ 06 6880 1094 🚌 To Corso Vittorio Emanuele II

Trinity college
Rome has several Irish-style pubs and bars. This is one of the better ones, with good-value food, as well as Guinness.

✉ Via del Collegio Romano ☎ 06 678 6472 🚌 To Via del Corso and Piazza Venezia

Northern Rome

This chapter encompasses two contrasting areas of Rome. The first is around Termini, the city's main railway station, a rather unlovely part of the city that you'd probably avoid were it not for a superb museum (the Palazzo Massimo alle Terme) and a major church (Santa Maria di Maggiore) which are situated here.

Villa Borghese

The second area within Northern Rome is based around Piazza di Spagna, an area full of wonderful streets, fantastic shops, quiet green spaces, memorable views and many compelling museums and galleries.

Situated between the two areas is Rome's famous Fontana di Trevi. Throw in a coin and you'll be sure to come back to this beautiful city.

ACCADEMIA DI SAN LUCA

Rome's academy of fine arts was founded by Pope Gregory XIII in 1577. It moved to its present site, the Palazzo Carpegna, in the 1930s when its previous home was cleared to make way for Via dei Fori Imperiali. The building has an unusual inclined spiral ramp (designed by Borromini), instead of stairs, to the upper levels. The collection is predominantly the work of academicians, or was presented by them, with plenty of fine portraits and still lifes. Highlights include a fresco fragment by Raphael, three works attributed to Titian and paintings by Guido Reni, Van Dyck and Angelica Kauffman, one of the few female academy members.

www.accademiadisanluca.it

✚ 8E ✉ Piazza dell'Accademia di San Luca 77 ☎ 06 679 8850 ⏰ Call for opening hours 🖐 Free Ⓜ Barberini 🚌 52, 53, 61, 62, 63, 71, 95, 116, 119, 175, 492, 630 to Via del Tritone

ARA PACIS AUGUSTAE

A modern glass pavilion on the banks of the Tiber houses some fine Roman sculpture. The Ara Pacis (altar of peace) was commissioned by the Senate in 13BC to celebrate the victories of Emperor Augustus in Spain and Gaul; the outer walls of the enclosure that surrounds it depict a procession in which the faces of the imperial family and other important Romans can be seen. The panels by the entrances represent symbolic moments from the history and mythology of Rome.

Behind the altar is the round mausoleum of Augustus, built by the forward-planning emperor in 28BC, 42 years before his death.

www.arapacis.it

✚ 7D ✉ Lungotevere in Augusta ☎ 06 8205 9127 ⏰ Tue–Sun 9–7 🖐 Moderate

BASILICA DI SANTA MARIA MAGGIORE

On entering you are confronted by the seemingly endless rows of the nave's columns, the sweep of the cosmati floor and a ceiling decorated with the first gold to be brought from the New World. The Sistine (1585) and Pauline (1611) side chapels have opulent works by the most important artists of the day (Maderno, Reni and Ponzio to name but a few). The mosaics are, however, the basilica's glory. On the nave, a fifth-century narrative of the Old Testament and, in the apse, a stunning Glorification of Mary (1295), to whom the church is dedicated, Our Lady herself indicating the site by sending the sign of snowfall in August, an event still celebrated every year. The façade (1743–50) has been restored to its full magnificence.

✚ 21G ✉ Piazza di Santa Maria Maggiore ☎ 06 483195 🕐 Apr–end Sep daily 7–7 or 8; Oct–end Mar daily 7–6:30 ✋ Church free; mosaics and museum inexpensive 🚇 Termini, Cavour 🚌 16, 70, 71, 75, 84, 360 to Piazza di Santa Maria Maggiore

CATACOMBE DI SANTA PRISCILLA

These are the most charming of Rome's many catacombs. The guided tour of the 50m (164ft) deep galleries, where 40,000 early Christians were laid to rest, is led by polyglot nuns and includes the earliest-known picture of the Virgin (second century AD) and a chapel with frescoes of Bible stories. Priscilla was the widow of a Christian who was martyred by Emperor Domitian.

www.catacombedipriscilla.com

✚ 11A (off map) ✉ Via Salaria 430 ☎ 06 8620 6272 🕐 Tue–Sun 8:30–12, 2:30–5; closed Jan ✋ Moderate 🚌 63, 92, 310 to Santa Priscilla

FONTANA DI TREVI

Even without Anita Ekberg, famous for the *Dolce Vita* scene in which she immerses herself in Trevi's turbulent waters, this effusively over-the-top fountain is a must for any visitor to Rome (and anyone wanting to return to the city should throw a coin into it). It was designed by Nicolò Salvi in 1762 and shows Neptune flanked by two massive steeds, representing the calm and stormy sea bursting out of an artificial cliff face. It contrasts beautifully with the calm orderliness of the Palazzo Poli, in whose wall it is built. The panels across the top depict the finding of the spring that feeds the ancient Roman canal leading into the fountain. By the way, the water is now said to contain bleach.

➕ 8E ✉ Piazza di Trevi 🚌 52, 53, 61, 62, 71, 95, 117, 119 and other buses to Via del Tritone and Via del Corso

GALLERIA BORGHESE

The sculpture collection, on the ground floor, includes some important classical works, such as a *Sleeping Hermaphrodite* and a

Dancing Faun, and the famous Canova sculpture of Paolina Bonaparte Borghese as a reclining Venus. The highlights, however, are the spectacular sculptures by Bernini. Cardinal Scipione Borghese, who had the villa and park built between 1608 and 1615, was Bernini's first patron. Here the sculptor's precocious talent is evident in works such as *The Rape of Proserpine*, *David* (thought to be a self-portrait) and *Daphne and Apollo*. The paintings are on the ground-floor walls and upstairs. Among the celebrated works are the *Deposition* by Raphael, Titian's early masterpiece *Sacred and Profane Love*, a restored *Last Supper* by Jacopo Bassano, now rich and vibrant, Correggio's erotic *Danae* and fine works by Guercino, Veronese, Giorgione and Andrea del Sarto. Caravaggio is represented here by six paintings, including one of his most important early works, the luscious *Boy with a Fruit Basket*, the *Sick Bacchus* and also the wonderfully realistic *Madonna of the Serpent*.

✚ 10B ✉ Piazzale del Museo Borghese 5 ☎ 06 841 7645 (recorded information) 🕑 Tue–Sun 9–7 ✋ Expensive 🍴 Bar Ⓜ Spagna/Flamino 🚌 52, 53, 910 to Via Pinciana ❓ Advance reservations on 06 32810 or online at www.ticketeria.it. There are guided tours every two hours in English and Italian

GALLERIA NAZIONALE D'ARTE MODERNA E CONTEMPORANEA

Cesare Bazzini's *Belle Epoque* palace is one of the few remaining buildings erected for the Rome International Exhibition of 1911 in the northwest area of the park of Villa Borghese. The collection covers the 19th and 20th centuries, mostly Italian artists – De Chirico, the Futurists and the *macchiaioli* (Italy's answer to the French Impressionists) – although there are also works by Gustav Klimt, Paul Cézanne and Henry Moore. Major temporary exhibitions are also staged. The museum has been extensively renovated, long-closed wings are being opened up, there is a new sculpture section and important contemporary acquisitions have been made.

🕂 8A 🖂 Viale delle Belle Arti 131
☎ Booking: 06 323 4000; www.gnam.arti.beniculturali.it
🕔 Tue–Sun 8:30–7:30 ✋ Moderate 🚌 Trams 19, 30B
to Viale delle Belle Arti

MUSEO CIVICO DI ZOOLOGIA

This museum, located alongside the city zoo or Bioparco (▶ 62), consists of the newly arranged civic zoological collection, following all the modern display criteria, and has an important animal and insect collection. Among the highlights are the extinct species and the display of shells. A visit here is an interesting diversion from the zoo itself.

www.comune.roma.it/museozoologia
🕂 9A 🖂 Via Ulisse Aldrovandi 18 ☎ 06 6710 9270
🕔 Tue–Sun 9–5 ✋ Moderate 🚌 52, 53, 910 to zoo in
Villa Borghese

MUSEO KEATS-SHELLEY

Since 1909 this house at the foot of the Spanish Steps, where Keats died of consumption at only 25 in February 1821, has been a memorial to Keats, Shelley, Byron and other Romantic poets. The rooms which Keats occupied on the first floor now contain a collection of manuscripts, documents and ephemera, including Keats's death mask and a lock of his hair. There is also an extensive specialist library. There is a Landmark Trust flat on the third floor available for rent.

www.keats-shelley-house.org

✚ 8D ✉ Piazza di Spagna 26 ☎ 06 678 4235 🕓 Mon–Fri 9–1, 3–6, Sat 11–4, 3–6 ✋ Inexpensive Ⓜ Spagna 🚌 119 to Piazza di Spagna

❓ Maximum of 15 people at one time

MUSEO NAZIONALE DELLE PASTE ALIMENTARI

This well-organized museum will tell you everything you ever needed to know about pasta (and a lot more besides). A portable CD player provides commentary (in Italian, English, Japanese, French or German) to the displays. The entire gamut of pasta production is covered, and there are examples of equipment and machinery used over the years, some rather questionable artworks on the pasta theme and photos of Italian and international personalities tucking into steaming plates of the nation's most-loved dish.

www.pastainmuseum.com

✚ 9E ✉ Piazza Scanderberg 117 ☎ 06 699 1119 🕓 Daily 9:30–5:30 ✋ Expensive 🚌 52, 53, 61, 62, 63, 71, 80, 160, 850 to Piazza San Silvestro

MUSEO NAZIONALE ROMANO

The museum is housed in two beautifully restored palaces, the **Palazzo Altemps,** a short distance from Piazza Navona, and the **Palazzo Massimo alle Terme,** near the station. The Altemps, one of Rome's finest Renaissance buildings, is a top-class assemblage of classical sculpture, mainly comprising the famous Cardinal Ludovico Ludovisi's collection, amassed in the 17th century. Note the beautiful fifth-century carved marble 'Ludovisi Throne' dedicated to Athena. Also housed here is the Egyptian collection of antiques and portraits. The beautiful baroque frescoes in the rooms make a wonderful backdrop for the sculpture.

The upper floors of the Palazzo Massimo are bursting with archaeological goodies from the Roman Age (second century BC to fourth century AD), such as the exquisite mosaics from Livia's palace and a superb

marble statue of a discus thrower (a Roman copy of a fifth-century BC Greek bronze). It is worth investing in the well-illustrated guidebook to negotiate your route around the extensive displays. Spacious and airy rooms open onto a courtyard, the exhibits are clearly labelled and each room has information sheets in English and Italian.

www.archeormiarti.benicultural.it

Palazzo Altemps

🕇 6E 🖂 Sant' Apollinare 44 ☎ 06 3996 7700 🕓 Tue–Sun 9–7:45 👋 Moderate 🚌 30, 70, 81, 116 to Corso del Rinascimento

Palazzo Massimo alle Terme

🕇 11E 🖂 Largo di Villa Peretti 1 ☎ 06 3996 7700 🕓 Tue–Sun 9–7:45 👋 Moderate 🚇 Termini 🚌 64 and all services to Termini

PALAZZO BARBERINI

Best places to see, ➤ 48–49.

PALAZZO DELLE ESPOSIZIONI

Rome's purpose-built (1883) palace of the fine arts has had a chequered history. Apart from serving its original brief, the building has housed the Communist Party, been a mess for Allied servicemen, a polling station and even a public toilet. After years of restoration it was relaunched in 1990 as a vibrant multi-media venue with a strong emphasis on film and video in addition to an active programme of Italian and international exhibitions (both historical and contemporary).

www.palazzoesposizioni.it

🕇 10F 🖂 Via Nazionale 194 ☎ 06 488 5465 🕓 Hours vary according to exhibition 🚇 Repubblica, Cavour 🚌 H, 40, 60, 64, 70, 117, 170 to Via Nazionale

PALAZZO DEL QUIRINALE

This large orange palace, with the picture-book round lookout tower to its left, is the official residence of the President of the Republic of Italy and is guarded by exotically uniformed *Granatieri*, who have been specially selected for their height and good looks. It was built in the 1570s as a papal summer palace offering fresh air on the highest of Rome's seven hills. Opposite, the two massive men with somewhat undersized horses are ancient Roman copies of a fifth-century BC Greek sculpture of Castor and Pollux, the two god-knights who came to Rome's rescue during an early battle. The palace is open to the public only on Sunday mornings, with the gardens open on 2 June, Italian Republic Day.

www.quirinale.it

✚ 9F ✉ Piazza del Quirinale ☎ 06 46991 🕔 Sun 8:30–12; closed Jul, Aug and most hols ✋ Moderate 🚌 40, 60, 64, 70, to Via IV Novembre

PIAZZA BARBERINI

The traffic-filled square at the foot of Via Vittorio Veneto, the street that was the hub of the *Dolce Vita* days of swinging Rome in the 1960s, contains two fountains designed by Bernini in the 1640s for the Barberini family. At the junction with Via Vittorio Veneto is the Fontana delle Api, whose grotesquely large bees (the Barberini family crest) crawl over the unassuming basin. In the middle of the square is the far more dramatic *Tritone*, whose well-muscled body is supported by his own fish-tail legs and four dolphins as he blows water through a vast seashell.

✚ 10E ✉ Piazza Barberini Ⓜ Barberini 🚌 61, 62, 175, 492 to Piazza Barberini

PIAZZA DEL POPOLO

For the Grand Tourists of the 18th and 19th centuries this was the first sight of Rome as their luggage-laden carriages trundled through the Porta del Popolo. It was also where criminals were executed (by having their heads smashed with hammers, until the guillotine took over in the early 19th century). It is overlooked to the east by the Pincio Gardens, which offer marvellous views. The two apparently identical churches at the end of Via del Corso were built in the late 17th century by Rainaldi; looks can deceive though and, to fit into the available space, one of them actually has an oval rather than a round dome. Domenico Fontana designed the fountain (1589) around the 3,000-year-old obelisk that Emperor Augustus brought from Egypt.

✚ 7C ✉ Piazza del Popolo 🚇 Flaminio 🚌 117, 119, 628, 926 to Piazza del Popolo

PIAZZA DELLA REPUBBLICA

This is a rather seedy square whose once elegant colonnade is now occupied by adult cinemas and tourist-trapping bars. One side is dominated by the third-century AD remains of the baths of Diocletian, into which Michelangelo incorporated the church of Santa Maria degli Angeli in 1563. The enticingly voluptuous nymphs (1901) of Mario Rutelli's *Fontana delle Naiadi* were greeted with scandalized horror when they were unveiled in 1910, but they have aged badly and their bodies are pock-marked by pollution.

🕇 11E ✉ Piazza della Repubblica 🚇 Repubblica
🚌 40, 64, 84, 86, 90, 170, 175, 492, 910, H to Piazza della Repubblica

PIAZZA DI SPAGNA

The sweeping Spanish Steps, designed in 1720 to connect the piazza with the French church of Trinità dei Monti, are now usually smothered with tourists, Italian soldiers and street vendors who compete for space with tubs of azaleas in springtime and a life-size nativity scene at Christmas. The piazza gets its name from the Spanish Embassy that was here in the 17th century, and has been a compulsory stop for visitors to Rome since the 18th and 19th centuries, when local tradesmen, models, unemployed servants and beggars mingled hopefully with the foreign artists, writers and Grand Tourists who congregated here. Keats lived and died in an apartment here (➤ 140–141). The low-lying

Fontana della Barcaccia (fountain of the broken boat) at the bottom of the steps was designed by Pietro Bernini, father of the more famous Gian Lorenzo, in 1627 for Barberini Pope Urban VIII; the bees and suns were taken from the Barberini family crest. Southeast, in Piazza Mignanelli, is a statue of the Virgin Mary on top of a column. This was erected in 1857, when Pope Pius IX proclaimed the doctrine of the Immaculate Conception, holding that the Virgin was the only person to have been born without original sin.

🞣 8D 🖂 Piazza di Spagna Ⓜ Spagna 🚌 119 to Piazza di Spagna

SANT'ANDREA AL QUIRINALE

This church is a theatrical Bernini gem (1628–70), decorated in pink marble. The portico beckons and the interior embraces soothingly. The oval space (imposed by site restrictions), the short distance between entrance and altar, the gold ceiling, dark chapels and four massive richly veined columns all combine to pull one's gaze to the altar and Cortese's marble-framed *Martyrdom* borne by angels. On the pediment above, St Andrew soars to heaven, while garlanded cherubs perch and fishermen recline. The architectural expression of Bernini's sculptural ideals, it was his personal favourite, built for no payment. Also worth noting are the walnut-lined sacristy and chapels of St Stanislao (paintings by Sebastiano del Pozzo, statues by Legros).

🞣 10E 🖂 Via del Quirinale 29 ☎ 06 474 4872 🕐 Daily 8–12, 4–7, but may vary 🚌 71, 1176 to Via Milano; 70, 117, 170 to Via Nazionale

SAN CARLO ALLE QUATTRO FONTANE

This was Borromini's first major work (1638) after a long apprenticeship under Maderno. It is difficult for modern eyes to appreciate the revolutionary quality of this tortured man's work. He overturned the Renaissance assumptions that architecture was based on the proportions of the human body, focusing instead on geometric units. The manipulation of the minuscule space is ingenious, not least in the swiftly shrinking coffers of the honeycombed dome, which give an illusion of size. The changing rhythms inside are also present on the façade, Borromini's last work (1667).

www.sancarlino-borromini.it

✚ 10E ✉ Via del Quirinale 23 (corner of Via Quattro Fontane) ☎ 06 488 3261 🕐 Mon–Fri 10–1, 3–6, Sun 10–1 🚇 Repubblica, Barberini 🚌 40, 60, 64, 70, 117, 170 to Via Nazionale

SANTA MARIA DELLA CONCEZIONE

If you feel like contemplating mortality then visit this little church (1631–38), a Barberini initiative for the Capuchin monks. The sombre theme is spelt out on the tombstone of a Barberini ('here lie dust, ashes and nothing'), but reaches a climax in the musty smell of the bone-lined crypt, where dead monks' remains decorate the ceiling and walls. The church is known for Guido Reni's painting St Michael Tempting the Devil, in which the Devil is reputedly a portrait of Pamphili Pope Innocent X.

✚ 9D ✉ Via Vittorio Veneto 27 ☎ 06 487 1185 🕐 Daily 7–12, 3 or 4–7 🚇 Barberini 🚌 52, 53, 95, 116, 119 to Via Veneto

SANTA MARIA DEL POPOLO

The church is bursting with masterpieces. Part of the façade and interior are by Bernini, whose Habbakuk and Daniel statues are cramped into small niches in the Renaissance Chigi Chapel (Raphael, 1516), along with mosaics. An angel visits Habbakuk and Daniel is praying with arms outstretched. Caravaggio and Carracci, the two dominant forces of baroque painting, are together in the Cerasi Chapel (left transept). Caravaggio's *Conversion of St Paul*,

so dramatically foreshortened that he seems to fall off the canvas, and the strong diagonals of the *Crucifixion of St Peter* share the space with Carracci's *Assumption of the Virgin* (1601). Pinturicchio (*c*1485), whose work can be seen in the frescoes, is represented by paintings in the Della Rovere Chapel.

The church is worth visiting for any one of these works; to have them all under one roof nestling against the Roman wall in this magnificent piazza is a treat indeed.

✚ 7C ✉ Piazza del Popolo 12 🕓 Mon–Sat 8–1:30, 4:30–7:30, Sun 8–7:30 🚇 Flaminio 🚌 117, 119 to Piazzale Flaminio

SANTA MARIA DELLA VITTORIA

You could be forgiven for leaving Santa Maria della Vittoria off a busy itinerary; its baroque façade and interior are not the best examples in Rome, despite having been worked on by the architects Maderno and Soria and containing paintings by Domenichino, Guercino and Reni. However, it does contain Bernini's Cornaro Chapel and his *Ecstasy of St Teresa*, one of the finest pieces of baroque sculpture, making the church well worth a detour. The restored *St Teresa* embodies Bernini's ideas of capturing the dramatic moment, in this case the saint's religious ecstasy (erotic to some modern perceptions) as the Cornaro cardinals look down from the side chapel.

✚ 10D ✉ Via XX Settembre 17 ☎ 06 4274 0571 🕓 Mon–Sat 8:30–12, 3:30–6; but hours may vary 🚇 Repubblica

SANTA PRASSEDE

Santa Prassede has mosaics unrivalled in medieval Rome. The figure of Christ dominates the vault, flanked by saints and Pope Paschal I (who built the church in AD817–824), distinguished by his square halo of the living. The apse mosaics are rich in symbols: the phoenix (resurrection), the eagle, ox, angel and lion (the evangelists) and the four rivers of Eden (earthly paradise). The glimmering intricacy of mosaics can be enjoyed up close in the side Chapel of St Zeno. Worth noting is a bust of Monsignor Giovanni Battista Santoni, carved by Bernini when a teenager.

✚ 21G ✉ Via di Santa Prassede 9a ☎ 06 488 2456 🕔 Daily 7:30–12, 4–6:30 🚇 Termini 🚌 16, 71, 75, 84 to Via Cavour-Piazza dell'Esquilino

SANTA PUDENZIANA

An early Christian basilica (AD401–17) was erected here over ancient Roman baths and a house but tradition supposes this to be the site of the oldest church in Rome (AD145). It has seen many changes over the centuries; witness the baroque opulence of the Caetani Chapel, through which you descend to reach the ancient remains; ask to see this. The main impact comes from the stunning fourth-century apse mosaics set in the nave's serene context.

✚ 11F ✉ Via Urbana 160 ☎ 06 481 4622 🕔 Mon–Sat 8–12, 3–6, Sun 3–6 🚇 Termini, Cavour 🚌 74, 84 to Via Cavour-Piazza dell'Esquilino; 70, 71 to Via A. de Pretis

VIA CONDOTTI

Usually packed with well-heeled shoppers and visitors, this elegant street is the heart of designer Rome, and most of the big Italian names have shops here or on the adjoining streets. It runs from Via del Corso to Piazza di Spagna and has an excellent view of the Spanish Steps.

✚ 8D ✉ Via Condotti 🚇 Spagna 🚌 117, 119 to Via Condotti

VILLA GIULIA

This charming palace, with its shady courtyards, houses the national collection of Etruscan art, although it was originally built in 1550–55 as a summer residence for Pope Julius III. The central loggia and *nymphaeum*, decorated with frescoes and mosaics, were frequently copied in later 16th-century Italian villas.

The Etruscans arrived in Italy towards the end of the eighth century BC and settled between the Arno and the Tiber, the area known as Etruria (present day Lazio, Umbria and southern Tuscany). The objects unearthed from Etruscan tombs in the region bear witness to the sophistication of the civilization. The highlight of the collection is the sixth-century BC terracotta sarcophagus of a husband and wife reclining on a divan, found at the necropolis of Cerveteri and known as the Sacrophagus of the Spouses. Have a look at some of the jewellery and you will see that design has not necessarily changed all that much since.

🚇 7A ✉ Piazzale di Villa Giulia 9 ☎ 06 322 6571; book online at www.ticketeria.it or by calling 06 824 620 🕐 Tue–Sun 8:30–7:30
💶 Moderate 🚈 Flamino 🚌 3, 19 to Viale delle Belle Arti

HOTELS

Canova (€€€)

This three-star, comfortably appointed hotel is in a lovely, quiet and safe street near Termini station at Santa Maria Maggiore.

✉ Via Urbana 10/a ☎ 06 487 3314; www.canovahotelroma.it 🚇 Cavour
🚌 To Via Cavour

Caravaggio (€€)

The lovely wooden-framed door gives the impression of a private club and the atmosphere of this refurbished, centrally located hotel is as welcoming as you might expect.

✉ Via Palermo 73 ☎ 06 485 915; www.caravaggio.com 🚇 Repubblica
🚌 To Via Nazionale

Corot (€€)

Right next to Termini station so perfectly placed for getting to all sights both in and out of town, this hotel offers comfortable rooms and a hospitable and multi-lingual staff.

✉ Via Marghera 15/17 ☎ 06 4470 0900; www.hotelcorot.it 🚇 Termini
🚌 To Termini

Elite (€€)

A moderately priced, very comfortable small hotel in an expensive area. It also has air-conditioning, an important consideration in central Rome in the summer.

✉ Via F. Crispi 49 ☎ 06 678 3083 🚇 Barberini 🚌 To Via del Tritone

Esquilino (€€)

On the 'clean' side of Termini station, this lovingly refurbished hotel is run by two professional hoteliers. Some rooms look out at Santa Maria Maggiore but the courtyard is quieter.

✉ Piazza dell'Esquilino 29 ☎ 06 474 3454 🚇 Termini 🚌 To Piazza dell'Esquilino

Excelsior, Westin (€€€)

Probably the most prestigious hotel in Rome, with a luxury and service reminiscent of the days before mass travel.

✉ Via Vittorio Veneto 125 06 47081; www.westin.com/excelsiorrome
Ⓜ Barberini 🚍 To Vittorio Veneto

Firenze (€€)
This hotel is on the first floor of a chic but busy street (near the Spanish Steps) so ask for a courtyard room.
✉ Via Due Macelli 106 ☎ 06 679 7240; www.hotelfirenzeroma.it
Ⓜ Barberini 🚍 To Via del Tritone

Hassler–Villa Medici (€€€)
One of the grandest old-style luxury hotels in the heart of the most elegant part of the city, with a view to die for from the elegant roof terrace.
✉ Piazza Trinità dei Monti 6 ☎ 06 699340; www.hotelhasslerroma.com
Ⓜ Spagna 🚍 To Via del Tritone

D'Inghilterra (€€€)
A very classy place, situated in a most elegant area of the city. Over a century old, it boasts former guests such as Hemingway and Liszt.
✉ Via Bocca di Leone 14 ☎ 06 699811; www.royaldemeure.com
🚍 To Piazza San Silvestro

La Residenza (€€)
Well-placed near Via Vittorio Veneto and Villa Borghese, this hotel evokes the atmosphere of an elegant private house. Stylish, spacious rooms plus a terrace and roof garden.
✉ Via Emilia 22/4 ☎ 06 488 0789; www.hotel-la-residenza.com
Ⓜ Barberini 🚍 To Via Vittorio Veneto

YOUTH HOSTELS
YWCA (€)
This hostel, near Termini station, is the perfect option if you are in Rome for early starts and serious sightseeing as there is an evening curfew.
✉ Via Cesare Balbo 4 ☎ 06 488 0460; www.ywca.ucdg.it Ⓜ Termini
🚍 To Via Cavour

RESTAURANTS

Agata e Romeo (€€€)

Near the Basilica of Santa Maria Maggiore, this intimate, elegant restaurant is renowned for its convivial atmosphere, its excellent Roman and southern Italian dishes and its good wine list.

✉ Via Carlo Alberto 45 ☎ 06 446 6115 🕐 Mon–Fri Ⓜ Vittorio Emanuele 🚌 70, 71, 360 to Via Carlo Alberto

Colline Emiliane (€€)

An old-fashioned family trattoria just off Piazza Barberini, which adheres strictly to the traditions of the rich cuisine of the northern region of Emilia Romagna. Excellent homemade pasta, particularly *tortellini*, boiled meats and no frills.

✉ Via degli Avignonesi 22 ☎ 06 481 7538 🕐 Tue–Sat lunch and dinner, Sun lunch only; closed Aug Ⓜ Barberini 🚌 To Piazza Barberini

Fiaschetteria Beltramme (€€)

Try to get here early after a shopping trip. A nostalgic survivor of past glories, this tiny trattoria is beginning to suffer from too much superstar visibility, so catch the lingering atmosphere. Share your table, jostle with the famous and enjoy genuine Roman cooking in suitably uninhibited, cramped conditions.

✉ Via della Croce 39 🕐 Mon–Sat Ⓜ Spagna 🚌 To Via del Corso

Gioia Mia (Pisciapiano) (€)

A useful spot after a hard day's shopping, offering menus for all palates and purses: from pizzas to full-blown meals. Noisy and chaotic but enjoyable nonetheless. (*Pisciapiano*, for those with linguistic curiosity, actually refers to a Tuscan wine with diuretic qualities, hence the emblematic cherub relieving himself.)

✉ Via degli Avignonesi 34 ☎ 06 488 2784 🕐 Mon–Sat Ⓜ Barberini 🚌 To Piazza Barberini

'Gusto (€–€€)

A chic, minimalist place that opened in the 1990s and is much loved by the Romans. Downstairs it's pizzas and salads, upstairs the restaurant combines Italian traditions with stir-fry Eastern cooking. Saturday and Sunday brunch is served 11:30–3:30. Be prepared for lunch-time office crowds.

✉ Piazza Augusto Imperatore 9 ☎ 06 322 6273 🕙 Daily 🚌 To Piazza Augusto Imperatore

Il Margutta (€–€€)

A good vegetarian restaurant and a place to drop in, at any time of day, for a drink, a snack or a complete meal. Good selection of Mediterranean vegetable dishes and a recommended delicate *fritto misto*. You can dine outside in fine weather.

✉ Via Margutta 118 ☎ 06 3265 0577 🕙 Daily 🚇 Flaminio
🚌 To Piazzale Flaminio

Otello alla Concordia (€€)

After some serious shopping in the busy Via del Corso relax in the attractive 18th-century courtyard of this family-run restaurant. Typical Roman fare is accompanied by some local wine. Book for outside tables.

✉ Via della Croce 81 ☎ 06 679 1178 🕙 Mon–Sat 🚇 Spagna 🚌 To Via del Corso

Papà Baccus (€€)

An eminently reliable, welcoming restaurant in the often-daunting Via Veneto area. From his native Tuscany, the owner offers traditional country soups, ham, salami, grilled meats and fish, and delicious homemade desserts. Service is informal and there are seats outside in summer.

✉ Via Toscana 36 ☎ 06 4274 2808 🕙 Mon–Fri lunch and dinner, Sat dinner only 🚇 Barberini 🚌 To Via Vittorio Veneto

Pizzaré (€)

This place is worth a stop, especially at lunchtime, for true large-format Neapolitan pizzas in nearly 40 different combinations. The set menus are at ludicrously low prices; also pasta, meat, salads and desserts.

✉ Via di Ripetta 14 ☎ 06 321 1468 🕙 Daily 🚌 To Lungotevere in Augusta

SHOPPING

ANTIQUES
Antichità
Located in an area with some interesting antiques shops, albeit pricey, Antichità specializes in old fabrics and furnishings.

✉ Via del Babuino 83/86 ☎ 06 320 7585 🚇 Spagna 🚌 To Piazzale Flaminio

ART
Alberto di Castro
Definitely the shop to visit for authentic prints. It stretches far back off the street and is lined with prints of all price ranges. There's a great selection of framed or unframed Roman scenes.

✉ Via del Babuino 71 ☎ 06 361 3752 🚇 Spagna 🚌 To Piazza San Silvestro, Via del Tritone

BOOKS
Mel Bookshop
One of the largest, newest bookshops in Rome. 'Mel' has a good English section. It sells everything from kids' books to CDs and even has a café in the art department.

✉ Via Nazionale 254/5 ☎ 06 488 5405 🚇 Repubblica 🚌 To Via Nazionale

Touring Viaggi
This bookshop and travel agent of the Touring Club Italiano stocks all you need in terms of maps and guides, as well as a small selection of tasteful postcards.

✉ Via del Babuino 20 ☎ 06 3600 5281 🚇 Spagna, Flaminio 🚌 To Piazzale Flaminio

CHILDREN'S CLOTHES
La Cicogna
Chic high-quality Italian kids' fashion and elegant yet practical maternity clothes, well-made but at somewhat high prices. You can get some great bargains if you catch the sales.

✉ Via Frattina 138 ☎ 06 679 1912 🚌 To Via del Corso

FASHION
Brioni
Located close to the famous Via Vittorio Veneto, Brioni has been dressing royalty and celebrities since 1945 and is regarded as one of Italy's top tailors. The suits and tuxedos reflect the highest standards of quality and craftsmanship. This, the largest branch, also has ready-to-wear for both men and women.

✉ Via Barberini 79 ☎ 06 484517 🚇 Barberini 🚌 To Via Barberini

Fendi
There are fur coats, shoes and ready-to-wear clothes, but it is the much-copied signature handbag, with the discreet 'F' in the design, that is the classic purchase for both Romans and visitors.

✉ Via Borgognona 36/40 ☎ 06 679 7641 🚇 Spagna 🚌 To Piazza di Spagna or Via del Corso

Giorgio Armani
The beautifully cut, hand-finished clothes of this Milanese designer can be found in the prestigious Via Condotti. Look for the slightly less expensive off-the-peg *Emporio* line, which is round the corner on Via del Babuino.

✉ Via Condotti 77 ☎ 06 699 1460 🚇 Spagna 🚌 To Via del Corso

Gucci
Another classic Italian fashion house offers inimitable wares in a soothing creamy-beige outlet on the most chic street in Rome.

✉ Via Condotti 8 ☎ 06 679 0405 🚇 Spagna 🚌 To Via del Corso

Missoni
The elegance of the knitwear is almost outrageous. The towels offer a taste of the style, if your budget can't stretch to a sweater.

✉ Piazza di Spagna 78 ☎ 06 679 2555 🚇 Spagna 🚌 To Via del Corso

Max Mara
The affordable end of designer land, Max Mara offers wonderfully crisp shapes and clean tones, in various branches.

✉ Via Condotti 167–69 ☎ 06 6992 2104 🚇 Spagna 🚌 To Via del Corso

Prada

Prestigious Italian fashion label based in Milan. Men and women's clothes, shoes and accessories.

✉ Via Condotti 92–95 ☎ 06 679 0897 Ⓜ Spagna 🚌 To Piazza di Spagna

Roberto Cavalli

A chic boutique owned by Italian fashion mogul Roberto Cavalli. Elegant designs in his own unique style.

✉ Via Borgognona 7a ☎ 06 6992 5469 Ⓜ Spagna 🚌 To Piazza di Spagna

Valentino

Rome's own has his boutique on Via Condotti, just two steps from the wonderful headquarters in Piazza Mignatelli.

✉ Via Condotti 13 ☎ 06 678 5862 Ⓜ Spagna 🚌 To Via del Corso

INTERIOR DESIGN
Frette

The queen of household linens and wonderful sleepwear. The bed linen and towels, often inspired by classical designs, are quite beautiful, as are the prices unless your trip happens to coincide with the sales.

✉ Via Nazionale 80 ☎ 06 488 2641 🚌 To Via Nazionale

Modigliani

Four levels make up this interesting store on Via Condotti. Modigliani creates ceramics, tableware and Murano glass objects for decoration and the table. Climb the crystal staircase while you are there.

✉ Via Condotti 24 ☎ 06 678 5653 Ⓜ Spagna 🚌 To Via del Corso

JEWELLERY
Bulgari

While France has Cartier, Italy has Bulgari. You'll find classic yet modern designs using the very best of materials, including diamonds, pearls and gold. There is also a selection of elegant watches.

✉ Via Condotti 10 ☎ 06 696261 Ⓜ Spagna 🚌 To Via del Corso

LEATHER
Catello D'Auria
A lovely little drawer-lined shop with a small but excellent selection of leather gloves; they also sell hosiery.

✉ Via Due Macelli 55 ☎ 06 679 3364 🚇 Spagna 🚌 To Via del Tritone

Red and Blue
An excellent place to go if you are looking for top-quality leatherwear in the classic styles.

✉ Via Due Macelli 57/8 ☎ 06 679 1933 🚇 Spagna 🚌 To Via del Tritone

SHOES
Dominici
A pristine, white-tiled shop where this Roman designer's shoes are displayed in neat rows. The prices are good and the styles a bit out of the ordinary, without being over the top.

✉ Via del Corso 14 ☎ 06 361 0591 🚌 To Via del Corso

Fausto Santini
The ultimate in modern Roman shoe design, Santini's styles are original and elegant, with nothing quite like them elsewhere.

✉ Via Frattina 120/21 ☎ 06 678 4114 🚇 Spagna 🚌 To Via del Corso

STATIONERY
Vertecchi
A serious and modern stationery shop selling an excellent selection of pens and writing paper, sometimes by the sheet. There is a large artist's section.

✉ Via della Croce 70 ☎ 06 679 0155 or 06 6919 0071 🚇 Flaminio 🚌 To Via del Corso

SWIMWEAR
Marissa Padovani
The ultimate place to buy swimming costumes – as well as a good range of ready-to-wear, you can have your bikini or one-piece made to measure.

✉ Via delle Carrozze 81 ☎ 06 679 3946 🚇 Spagna 🚌 To Via del Corso

ENTERTAINMENT

CINEMA
Warner Village Moderno

There are five large screens in this ultra-modern complex, which sometimes shows new releases in English. Expect great sound and comfy seats.

✉ Piazza della Repubblica 45/6 ☎ 06 4777 9209 🚇 Repubblica 🚌 To Piazza della Repubblica

MUSIC
Teatro dell'Opera

The winter season of the Rome opera and ballet company takes place here. In summer (mid-Jun and Aug) performances are often staged in the Piazza di Siena, in the Villa Borghese.

✉ Via Firenze 72 ☎ 06 4816 0255/481 7003; www.opera.roma. it 🚇 Termini 🚌 To Termini

NIGHTLIFE
Alien

Vast mainstream disco with *cubistes* (scantily clad girls, and a few boys, who dance on top of columns for those who cannot be bothered to move themselves).

✉ Via Velletri 13 ☎ 06 841 2212 🚌 To Piazza Fiume

Gregory's

Drink Guinness while you indulge in some good live jazz. A pleasant venue near the Spanish Steps.

✉ Via Gregoriana 54d ☎ 06 679 6386 🕐 Tue–Sat 🚇 Barberini 🚌 To Piazza di Spagna

SPORT
Roman Sport Centre

Daily membership allows you access to the gyms of one of Rome's most exclusive sports and fitness clubs.

✉ The car park underneath Villa Borghese ☎ 06 320 1667/321 8096; www.romansportcentre.com 🕐 Mon–Sat 9am–10pm, Sun 9–3 🚇 Spagna 🚌 To Via Vittorio Veneto

Vatican City

The Vatican, the world's
smallest independent state,
contains two of the highlights
of any visit to Rome: the immense
Basilica di San Pietro, or St Peter's, and the vast Musei
Vaticani, or Vatican Museums, home to one of the
world's richest and largest collection of paintings,
sculptures and other works of art accumulated by the
papacy over the centuries.

CITTÀ DEL
VATICANO

BASILICA DI SAN PIETRO
Best places to see, ➤ 36–37.

CASTEL SANT'ANGELO
Best places to see, ➤ 40–41.

MUSEI VATICANI
Visiting the Vatican Museums can pose something of a
challenge, and not just because they are so large: opening
hours vary from year to year, as does the order in which
you are able to walk around. One-way systems introduced
at the busiest times of year can also make it difficult to
retrace your steps. The most popular sights – the Cappella
Sistina (Sistine Chapel, ➤ 38–39) and Stanze di Raffaello
(Raphael Rooms, ➤ 168–169) – are also the ones that are
farthest from the museum entrance. Try to see these first
if you arrive early – you'll avoid the queues. Otherwise
head first for the Museo Pio-Clementino (➤ 165).
www.vatican.va

✚ 2D ✉ Viale Vaticano ☎ 06 6988 3333 🕓 Mar to end Oct
Mon–Fri 10–4:45, Sat 10–1:45; Nov–end Feb Mon–Sat 10–1:45. Last
Sun of each month 10–1:45 💷 Expensive, but covers all Vatican museums
🚇 Ottaviano 🚌 23, 32, 49, 81, 492, 990 to Piazza del Risorgimento

Appartamento Borgio
This suite of apartments within the Vatican Museums was built
for Pope Alexander VI, a member of the notorious Borgia family,
during his papacy (1492–1503). Almost a palace within a palace, it
proved so sumptuous that subsequent popes chose to use it as
their principal lodgings for the next hundred years. Room 1, the
Sala delle Sibille, is where the infamous Cesare Borgia is said to
have had Alfonso of Aragon, the husband of his sister, Lucretia
Borgia, murdered. Today the room is better known for its frescoes,
created between 1492 and 1495 by Umbrian artist Pinturicchio.

Biblioteca Apostolica Vaticana

The Vatican library easily rates as the world's most valuable collection of books and manuscripts. Books were accumulated by the popes for centuries, but only found a permanent home in 1474 during the papacy of Sixtus IV. The collection includes some 100,000 manuscripts, 70,000 archive volumes, 800,000 printed works, 100,000 prints and maps and around 75,000 handwritten and illustrated books. Only a fraction of the collection is displayed here, but all the items are beautiful, and some – such as handwritten material by Michelangelo, Martin Luther, Petrarch and others – are of immense historical importance.

Cappella Sistina
Best places to see, ➤ 38–39.

Galleria delle Carte Geographique
This 120m-long (394ft) gallery on the upper floor of the museum complex is lined with intricately painted 16th-century maps of Italy, which were commissioned by Pope Gregory XIII. A richly decorated vaulted ceiling completes the jaw-dropping effect.

Museo Gregoriano-Etrusco
This 18-room museum is excellent if your interest in the Etruscans – who dominated central Italy before the rise of Rome – is not enough to take you all the way to the much larger Etruscan collection of the Villa Giulia (➤ 151). Like the Villa Giulia, this museum has its fair share of urns and vases, but it also contains

some of the greatest of all the Etruscan artefacts surviving today. The most celebrated of these is the *Mars of Todi* (Room III), a large bronze statue named after the Umbrian town in which it was found. Also worth special attention are the exhibits of Room II, most of which were taken from the Regolini-Galassi Tomb (*c*650BC) uncovered in 1836 at Cerveteri, just north of Rome. Like the Egyptians, the Etruscans buried the deceased with everyday items they might need in the afterlife, thereby providing archaeologists with a graphic picture of their domestic and artistic habits. The Etruscans arrived in Italy towards the end of the eighth century BC and lived in the area now encompassing Lazio, Umbrio and southern Tuscany.

Museo Pio-Clementino

The pick of the Vatican's classical sculpture collection is held in the Museo Pio-Clementino and its Cortile Ottagono, an octagonal courtyard containing some of the greatest of all classical sculptures.The most famous sculpture here is the *Laocoön*, an intricately carved sculptural group dating from around 50BC. Created by sculptors from Rhodes, it was found near the Domus Aurea (► 78) in 1506 and was identified from a description by the first-century scholar Pliny. The sculpture had a huge influence on Renaissance sculptors, especially Michelangelo. It shows a Trojan priest, Laocoön, and his two sons fighting with sea serpents sent by Apollo, after warning of the perils of the legendary wooden horse. Other works in the Cortile include the *Apollo del Belvedere*, a Roman copy of a fourth-century BC Greek bronze, a masterpiece of classical sculpture, which also greatly influenced Renaissance sculptors. The statue of the young god Apollo originally held a bow in one hand, and most likely an arrow in the other.

Beyond the Cortile lies the Sala degli Animali, a collection of ancient and 18th-century sculpted animals. Moving on, you come to the Galleria delle Statue, where the highlights are the *Apollo Sauroktonos*, a Roman copy of a fourth-century BC original showing Apollo about to kill a lizard, and the famed *Candelabri Barberini*, a pair of second-century lamps discovered at Hadrian's villa in Tivoli.

The Sala delle Muse is dominated by the *Torso del Belvedere*, probably a first-century BC Greek work. This gigantic torso was admired by Michelangelo, whose nudes in the Sistine Chapel frescoes were influenced by it. Visit the Sala a Croce Greca to see the Sarcofago di Sant'Elena and Sarcofago di Constantina, the sarcophagi – respectively – of the mother and daughter of Emperor Constantine.

Pinacoteca Vaticana

Even on its own, the Vatican's Pinacoteca, or picture gallery, would be considered one of Rome's best painting collections, with works from the early and High Renaissance to the 19th century. Its 16 rooms offer a chronological insight into the development of religious art, and would be richer still had Napoleon not pilfered many of their treasures at the beginning of the 19th century.

Room I opens with 11th-, 12th- and 13th-century Tuscan and Umbrian works. This is followed in Room II by one of the gallery's highlights – Giotto's *Stefaneschi Triptych* (c1315), which shows the *Martyrdom of SS Peter and Paul*. The triptych shows St Peter crucified upside-down, as he felt unworthy to die in the same way as Christ. Commissioned by Cardinal Stefaneschi, it was originally intended for one of the principal altars in the old St Peter's. The cardinal is depicted on either side of the Triptych.

Among the gallery's other star attractions are a majestic collection of works by Raphael in Room VIII, including the *Transfiguration* (1517–20). Unfinished at the artist's death, the work was hung over his coffin at his funeral and later completed by his pupils. Also in this room is Raphael's *Madonna of Foligno* (1512–13), which was commissioned as a votive offering in gratitude for a lucky escape during a seige. You can also see tapestries, woven in Brussels, based on Raphael's drawings, which were once displayed in the Sistine Chapel. Leonardo da Vinci's unfinished *St Jerome* hangs in Room IX, one of the few works attributed to him without dispute of authorship. Also in this room is the wonderful *Pietà* by Venetian artist Giovanni Bellini. There are more Venetian works in Room X, with two paintings by Titian: the *Portrait of Doge Nicolò Marcello* and the radiant *Madonna with Saints*.

These are just a few highlights among many, for the gallery possesses works by most leading Italian painters: Fra Angelico, Caravaggio, Veronese and a great many others.

Stanze di Raffaello

Raphael was just 37 at his death and painted relatively little. This makes the Stanze di Raffaello, or Raphael Rooms, which are almost entirely covered in frescoes by the painter, one of Italy's most treasured artistic ensembles. The four rooms were commissioned by Pope Julius II in 1508 and were completed after

the painter's death in 1520 by his pupils. They include scenes inspired by Leo X, who became pope while work was in progress.

The order in which you're allowed to see the rooms varies from month to month, but if possible try to see them in the order in which they were painted. The Stanza della Segnatura (1508–11) served as Julius's library and was the place where he applied his signature *(segnatura)* to papal bulls (edicts). The frescoes here are the rooms' finest – many critics call them an even greater achievement than the Sistine Chapel. The four main pictures represent the humanist ideals of theology, philosophy, poetry and justice in a complicated allegorical manner; it is well worth buying a guide to help decipher the paintings.

The next room to be painted was the Stanza di Eliodoro (1512–14). The paintings here are a form of visual propaganda for Julius and Leo, but ostensibly show the timely intervention of Divine Providence in defence of an endangered faith. The battle scenes in *The Expulsion of Heliodorus* – a reworking of a biblical story – are an allusion to Julius' skill in defending the Papal States from foreign interference. Similarly, the panel showing Attila the Hun turning back from Rome actually contains a portrait of the new pope, Leo X (the figure on a donkey). *The Deliverance of St Peter from Prison* was the first time Raphael attempted to portray a scene set at night.

The third room chronologically was the Stanza dell' Incendio (1514–17), designed as a dining room for Leo X, who asked Raphael to paint a series of scenes that celebrated the achievements of two of his papal namesakes, Leo III and Leo IV. *The Fire in the Borgo* shows Leo IV – painted here as Leo X – extinguishing a fire near St Peter's by making the sign of the Cross.

Much of the Stanza dell'Incendio was painted by pupils working to designs by Raphael, as were the frescoes in the last room, the Stanza di Costantino (1517–24).

Before moving on from the Raphael Rooms, visit the nearby Cappella di Niccolò V, a small chapel that is covered in frescoes by Fra Angelico on the *Lives of St Stephen and St Lawrence* (1447–51).

HOTELS

Della Conciliazione (€€)

Situated in one of the lovely streets tucked away behind the Vatican. The rooms are a little small but they are pleasantly furnished. Friendly service from a multi-lingual staff.

✉ Via Borgo Pio 163/166 ☎ 06 686 7910; www.hotelconciliazione.com 🚇 To Piazza del Risorgimento

Emmaus (€€)

This fourth-floor 28-room hotel (some of the rooms have a view of St Peter's dome) is excellent value for this category. It has satellite TV and, unusually, wheelchair access.

✉ Via delle Fornaci 23 ☎ 06 635 658; www.emmaushotel.com 🚇 To Via Gregorio VII

RESTAURANTS

Borgo Nuovo (€€)

This restaurant, close to St Peter's, offers generous portions of tasty, freshly prepared Italian food. There are good choices for vegetarians, as well as plenty of fish and meat dishes.

✉ Borgo Pio 104 ☎ 06 689 2852 🕓 Wed–Mon 🚇 Ottaviano 🚇 To Piazza del Risorgimento

Roof Garden 'Les Etoiles' (€€€)

Wonderful Mediterranean cuisine and a superb view of St Peter's are on offer here – for a price. Eat on the roof terrace or in the elegant dining room.

✉ Via dei Bastioni 1 ☎ 06 687 3233 🕓 Daily 🚇 Ottaviano 🚇 To Piazza del Risorgimento

Taverna Angelica (€€)

A restaurant near St Peter's for romantic, intimate, candle-lit dining. Creative regional cuisine, both fish and meat, excellent cheeses and imaginative desserts (with well-matched dessert wines by the glass). Courteous and efficient service.

✉ Piazza delle Vaschette 14a ☎ 06 687 4514 🕓 Mon–Sat dinner only, Sun lunch and dinner 🚇 Ottaviano 🚇 To Piazza del Risorgimento

SHOPPING

FASHION
Gente

One of the best women's clothes shops in Rome, on one of the city's most popular shopping streets. Gente sells lots of wearable styles (including many designer labels). There are other branches in the central area.

✉ Via Cola di Renzo 277 ☎ 06 321 1516 🚌 To Piazza Cavour

JEWELLERY
Raggi

A fine shop for its wide selection at reasonable prices, with several branches in the city. This branch is on one of the best shopping streets in Rome.

✉ Via Cola di Rienzo 250 ☎ 06 689 6601 🚌 To Piazza Cavour

SOUVENIRS AND RELIGIOUS GIFTS
Galleria Savelli

Founded by Lorenzo Savelli in 1898, this family-owned shop still sells religious artefacts close to St Peter's. There is also a new showroom for mosaics in Via Paolo.

✉ Piazza Pio XII 1–2 ☎ 06 6880 6383 🚌 To Piazza del Risorgimento

Soprani

One of the many shops around the Vatican dedicated to serious religious objects and more commercially minded souvenirs of your trip to the Holy City; images of the Pope and Christ can be printed on almost everything.

✉ Via del Mascherino 29 ☎ 06 6880 1404 🚌 To Piazza del Risorgimento

ENTERTAINMENT

NIGHTLIFE
Fonclea

This long-established pub-club offers a wide variety of jazz, blues, Latin and other live music, most days.

✉ Via Crescenzio 82a ☎ 06 689 6302 🕐 Open until 2 or 3am 🚌 Bus to Piazza Cavour

Excursions

Just as all roads lead to Rome, they also lead from it. If you want to escape the chaos, crowds or summer heat, dozens of destinations are within easy reach.

To the southwest are the fascinating excavations of Ostia Antica. To the southeast the Castelli Romani offer a fine combination of history and gastronomy, while to the northwest the tombs of the Etruscans are waiting to be discovered. Viterbo, to the north, offers medieval charm, hot springs and Renaissance architectural extravagances, while you can only marvel at the extensive ruins of Hadrian's villa to the east.

Stopping for lunch at a local trattoria or selecting ingredients for a gourmet picnic is half the fun. But beware if you are driving, especially on Sundays. Romans are addicted to what they refer to as the *gita fuori porta,* or day trip out of town, and the traffic returning from these outings can be a nightmare.

CERVETERI

Founded by the Etruscans in the eighth century BC, ancient Caere was one of the great trading hubs of the Mediterranean between the seventh and fifth centuries BC. In the **Banditaccia Necropolis,** a couple of kilometres from the main piazza of modern Cerveteri, the tombs of the inhabitants of the prosperous city are laid out in the form of a town, with streets and squares – a real city of the dead.

A map on sale at the entrance to the necropolis, which is set among Roman pines and cypress trees, is a useful guide to the tombs. Do not miss the sixth-century Tomba dei Capitelli, carved from light volcanic rock to resemble Etruscan houses, and the Tomba dei Rilievi, decorated with painted reliefs of cooking utensils and other household objects. The Tomba degli Scudi e delle Sedie, outside the main gate, has chairs carved out of the tufo and unusual reliefs of shields decorating the walls.

The **Museo Nazionale di Cerveteri,** in the heart of the town, displays interesting pottery and sarcophagi from Cerveteri and the nearby port of Pyrgi, although most of the best discoveries are in the Museo Gregoriano-Etrusco, in the Vatican Museums (➤ 164–165), and at Villa Giulia (➤ 151).

Banditaccia Necropolis/Museo Nazionale di Cerveteri

☎ 06 994 0001 ⚅ Banditaccia Necropolis: Tue–Sun 8:30 to 1 hour before sunset. Museo Nazionale: Tue–Sun 8:30–7:30 ⚇ Necropolis and museum moderate ▤ COTRAL bus from Lepanto ▤ From Termini, Tiburtina, Ostiense or Trastevere to Cerveteri-Ladispoli station (6km/4 miles from heart of town) ▤ Bus runs from main piazza in Cerveteri to necropolis in summer only. **By car:** 44km (27 miles) by A12 or Via Aurelia (SS1)

FRASCATI

Situated 25km (16 miles) from Rome, Frascati is the nearest of the Castelli Romani – the towns dotted along the volcanic Alban Hills. Frascati suffered severe damage during World War II, but many of the buildings have been restored, including the cathedral of San Pietro in Piazza San Pietro and the church of Il Gesù, designed by Pietro da Cortona, which is decorated with fresco perspectives.

Frascati is renowned for both its white wine (this can be sampled fresh from the barrel in the numerous cellars around the town) and its Renaissance villas. The magnificent **Villa Aldobrandini,** designed by Giacomo della Porta between 1598 and 1603 for Cardinal Pietro Aldobrandini, a nephew of Pope Clement VIII, dominates the town. On a clear day the views of Rome from the terrace are breathtaking.

Frascati, with other Castelli towns, was once part of the ancient city of Tusculum, which dates back as far as the ninth century BC. It was a popular spot for Roman dignitaries, many of whom had villas there. The archaeological remains of Tusculum are scant:

there is a Roman road leading up to the former city, the ruins of the villa of Emperor Tiberius and – best-preserved of all – a small amphitheatre, now somewhat notorious after reports of black masses being held there.

Villa Aldobrandini

✉ Piazza G. Marconi, Frascati ☎ 06 942 0331 🕓 Mon–Fri 9–1, 3–6 (closes at 5 Oct–end Mar), Sat 9–1 🚆 Train from Termini station, 30 min. **By car**: Via Tuscolana from Rome for about 25km (16 miles) 👆 Free (the tourist office in Piazza G Marconi issues passes to the garden of Villa Aldobrandini)

ℹ Piazza Marconi 1, Frascati ☎ 06 942 0331

OSTIA ANTICA

Founded at the mouth of the river Tiber by the Romans in the fourth century BC, Ostia Antica was the port of ancient Rome, a key place for defence and trade until the fourth century AD.

After Pompeii and Herculaneum, Ostia Antica is the best-preserved Roman town in Italy. Its park-like setting is a refreshing change from the chaos of Rome. Allow a good few hours to explore the **excavations,** which are as fascinating (if not quite so

grand) as those at the Roman Forum and give a good impression of life in a working Roman town was like.

The ruins span both sides of the kilometre-long main street, the Decumanus Maximus, from the Porta Romana to the Porta Marina at the other end (which once opened onto the seafront). On the right just after the Porta Romana are the Terme di Nettuno (Baths of Neptune), best viewed by climbing the stone stairs at the front. Farther on is the amphitheatre, which could hold 2,700 people. It is used as a theatre in summer. Behind this is the commercial area, Piazzale delle Corporazioni, surrounded by offices and shops with vibrant mosaics announcing the trades practised by each business.

Back on the Decumanus Maximus, the ruins of the forum are to the left. Off to the right are the remains of some *horrea* (warehouses). Also on the right is the well-preserved Casa di Diana and the Thermopilium, a Roman bar complete with a marble counter and frescoes of the available fare. Just beyond, to the northeast, is the museum.

Before you leave, look at the medieval *borgo* (village) of Ostia, a stone's throw from the archaeological site.

✉ Viale degli Romagnoli 717 ☎ 06 5635 8099 🕓 Apr–end Sep Tue–Sun 9–6; Oct–end Mar Tue–Sun 8:30–4 👋 Moderate 🍴 Il Monumento (€€, ➤ 183) 🚇 Metro B to Piramide, then trains from adjoining railway station every 10–30 minutes to Ostia Antica. **By car:** 25km (16 miles). Via del Mare (SS8 bis) from Rome

TIVOLI

Tivoli was a country retreat for Roman patricians and a summer playground for the monied classes during the Renaissance. The Villa d'Este and Villa Adriana are the best-known sights, but it is worth having a look at the Rocca Pia, a 15th-century castle built by Pope Pius II at the top of the town, and wandering around the labyrinthine streets of the historical heart of town, stopping at the Romanesque church of San Silvestro (where there are some interesting early medieval frescoes) and the 17th-century cathedral of San Lorenzo.

There is a sense of faded splendour about the Renaissance pleasure palace **Villa d'Este,** created in 1550 by Cardinal Ippolito d'Este, grandson of Borgia Pope Alexander VI. The residence is totally upstaged by the gardens – an almost entirely symmetrical series of terraces, shady pathways and spectacular fountains. From 1865 to 1886 the villa was home to Franz Liszt and inspired his *Fountains of the Villa d'Este.*

The waterfalls and gardens of Tivoli's **Villa Gregoriana** were created when Pope Gregory XVI diverted the flow of the Aniene river to put an end to the periodic flooding in the area. There are two main waterfalls: the large Grande Cascata on the far side and a smaller one at the neck of the gorge, designed by Bernini.

Metro to Rebibbia, then COTRAL bus to Tivoli. Buses leave every 10 minutes (Mon–Sat), 15–20 minutes (Sun). **By car:** 40km (25 miles) east of Rome on Via Tiburtina SS5 or Rome-L'Aquila autostrada A24

Villa d'Este

Piazza Trento ☎ 0774 312070; www.villadestetivoli.info

May–Aug Tue–Sun 8:30–6:45; times may vary Expensive

Villa Gregoriana

Largo S Angelo ☎ 06 3996 7701; www.villasangregoriana.it

Apr to mid-Oct Tue–Sun 10–6:30; Mar, mid-Oct–Nov Tue–Sun 10–2:30; Dec, Feb by appointment only Moderate

VILLA ADRIANA

Constructed between AD118 and 134, the Villa Adriana was the largest and most sumptuous villa ever built in the Roman Empire. It was the country palace of Emperor Hadrian, and was later used by other emperors. After the fall of the empire it was plundered for building materials. Many of its decorations were used to embellish the Villa d'Este (➤ 178).

The site is enormous and you will need several hours to see it properly. Hadrian travelled widely and was a keen architect, and parts of the villa were inspired by buildings he had seen around the world. The Pecile, through which you enter, was a reproduction of a building in Athens and the Canopus, on the far side of the site, is a copy of the sanctuary of Serapis near Alexandria – the long canal of water represents the Nile.

Highlights include the fishpond, encircled by an underground gallery where the emperor took his walks, the baths and Hadrian's private retreat, the Teatro Marittimo, a small circular palace on an island in a pool, which could be reached only by a retractable bridge. There are *nymphaeums*, temples, barracks and a museum. Archaeologists have found features such as a heated bench with steam pipes under the sand, and a network of subterranean service passages for horses and carts.

✉ Via di Villa Adriana, Tivoli ☎ 0774 530203 🕐 Apr, Sep daily 9–7; May–Aug daily 9–7.30, Oct daily 9–6:30; Nov–Jan daily 9–5. Last ticket one hour before closing ✋ Expensive 🚌 32km (20 miles). Bus from Tivoli's Piazza Garibaldi to Villa Adriana. COTRAL bus can drop you on main road to Rome (1km/0.5 miles) to villa. **By car:** take A24 northeast, then Tivoli exit

VITERBO

Founded by the Etruscans and later taken over by Rome, Viterbo developed into an important medieval centre and in the 13th century became the residence of the popes. Although badly bombed during World War II, it remains Lazio's best preserved medieval town and its historical quarter, San Pellegrino, is such a perfect architectural ensemble that it is often used as a movie set. The natural hot springs close by are an additional attraction.

From the rather oddly named but lovely Piazza della Morte (Death Square), a bridge leads over to Piazza San Lorenzo and the black-and-white striped cathedral of the same name, which dates from the 12th century. Inside are magnificent cosmati tiled floors and the tomb of Pope John XXI. Next door is the 13th-century Palazzo Papale. Have a peek at the 'new' roof. The original one was removed in 1271, during the first conclave in Viterbo, to speed up the election of the pope.

The pretty Romanesque church of Santa Maria Nuova, with its outdoor pulpit from which St Thomas Aquinas preached, is also worth a look, before you head up to Piazza del Plebiscito, dominated by the 16th-century Palazzo Comunale. Stop for a rest in Piazza delle Erbe by the fountain or for refreshments at the 15th-century Caffè Schenardi.

🚌 COTRAL bus from Saxa Rubra station to Viterbo

🚆 From Termini station (also Tiburtina, Ostiense, Trastevere stations) to Viterbo (2 hours). **By car:** Cassia bis (SS2 bis) from Rome 110km/68 miles (1.5 hours)

HOTELS

TIVOLI
Delle Terme (€€)
This three-star hotel, with its own gardens and restaurant, is well placed for the villas of Tivoli.
✉ Piazza Bartolomeo della Quiete 5 ☎ (0774) 371033; www.hoteltermetivoli.it 🚊 To Tivoli

LA TORRACCIA
Hotel la Torraccia (€€)
A hotel which is not-too-distant from Rome and near the Estruscan ruins. Every room has a terrace.
✉ Viale Mediterraneo 45, Tarquinia Lido ☎ (0766) 864 375/8642; www.torraccia.it 🚊 To Tarquinia

CAMPSITES

Castelfusano Country Club (€)
This is one of the two campsites near the not-so-clean but long and wide Roman beaches. Rome is easily reached by public transportation. Open all year.
✉ Piazza di Castelfusano 1, Ostia ☎ 06 5618 5490/1; www.countryclubcastelfusano.it 🚊 To Castelfusano

Parco del Lago (€)
A tranquil campsite on the edge of Lake Bracciano. All necessary amenities, and popular with Romans, who come to get away from it all. Reserve early. Available in summer only.
✉ Lungolago di Polline 75, Strada Provinciale Anguillara–Trevignano Km 4,100 ☎ 06 9980 2003; www.parcodellago.com 🚊 To Anguillara/Trevignano

RESTAURANTS

FRASCATI
Cacciani (€€€)
Consistently reliable and spacious restaurant in the Castelli Romani with a large panoramic terrace. Classic meat and fish dishes from Rome and Lazio. Try the regional white Frascati wine.
✉ Via A. Diaz 15 ☎ 06 940 1991 🕐 Tue–Sat lunch and dinner, Sun lunch only

Zarazá (€–€€)
Simpler than Cacciani, featuring good traditional, regional fare.
✉ Via Viale Regina Margherita 45 ☎ 06 942 2053 🕐 Tue–Sat lunch and dinner, Sun lunch only

OSTIA ANTICA
Il Monumento (€€)
Well-made seafood dishes are served here and the special, *spaghetti monumento*, is a great mix of seafood and prawns.
✉ Piazza Umberto I 18 ☎ 06 565 0021 🕐 Tue–Sat

SPERLONGA
Agli Archi (€€€)
All the dishes at this little restaurant are delicious, from the *antipasto* of hot and cold seafood to the homemade desserts.
✉ Via Ottaviano 17 ☎ 0771 548300 🕐 Thu–Tue, daily in Jul and Aug

TIVOLI
Ristorante Antiche Terme di Diana (€€)
Well-established restaurant in the attractive cellar of an old building. The pasta is freshly made on the premises and the menu has wholesome and traditional dishes.
✉ Via Sose ☎ 0774 335239 🕐 Daily

VILLA ADRIANA
Adriano (€€–€€€)
One of the best options on the road to the Villa Adriana; you can sit outside in summer and enjoy a varied menu.
✉ Via di Villa Adriana 194 ☎ 0774 382235 🕐 Daily

VITERBO
Richiastro (€)
Traditional local dishes that you will not find in many other places, using simple ingredients such as bread with a spread made from eggs and peppers, lentil and chick-pea soups and tripe.
✉ Via della Marrocca 16–18 ☎ 0761 228009 🕐 Thu–Sat lunch and dinner, Sun lunch only

Index

Street index

Acknowledgements

The Automobile Association would like to thank the following photographers, companies and picture libraries for their assistance in the preparation of this book.
Abbreviations for the picture credits are as follows – (t) top; (b) bottom; (c) centre; (l) left; (r) right; (AA) AA World Travel Library.

4l/6/7 View over Giancolo, AA/S McBride; **4c** Colosseum, AA/S McBride; **4r** Colosseum, AA/A Kouprianoff; **5l** Pincio Gardens, AA/A Kouprianoff; **5c** Santa Maria Maggiore, AA/S McBride; **5r** Villa Adriana, AA/S McBride; **8/9** Vatican Musuem, AA/S McBride; **10/11** Castel Sant'Angelo, AA/S McBride; **10c** Frescoes, Villa Farnesina, AA/J Holmes; **10bl** St Peter's Basilica, AA/S McBride; **10br** Sistine Chapel, AA/S McBride; **11ct** Fontana dei Quattro Fuimi, Piazza Navona, AA/S McBride; **11cb** Colosseum, AA/A Kouprianoff; **11b** Scooter, AA/J Holmes; **12/13t** Icecream, AA/A Sawyer; **12/13b** Esquiline Market, AA/C Sawyer; **12c** Pasta, AA/T Souter; **12bl** Campo de' Fiori, AA/C Sawyer; **13c** Butcher's, AA/C Sawyer; **13b** Pizzeria, AA/C Sawyer; **14t** Artichokes, AA/C Sawyer; **14b** Wine bottles, AA/C Sawyer; **15t** Waiter, AA/C Sawyer; **15c** Coffee, AA/M Jourdan; **15b** Dolce Roma bakery, AA/C Sawyer; **16/17t** Sistine Chapel, AA/S McBride; **16/17b** Foro Romano, AA/S McBride; **17** Piazza di Spagna, AA/S McBride; **18t** The Colosseum; AA/S McBride; **18b** Fontana di Trevi, AA/S McBride; **19** Pantheon, AA/S McBride; **20/21** Colosseum, AA/S McBride; **26** Leonardo da Vinci Airport, AA/T Harris; **27** Stazione Termini, AA; **28** Foro Romano, bus, AA/S McBride; **29** Parking, Rome, AA/C Sawyer; **31** Pharmacy sign, AA/C Sawyer; **34/35** Colosseum, AA/A Kouprianoff; **36/37** Basilica di San Pietro over the Tiber, AA/C Sawyer; **37** St Peter's Basilica, AA/S McBride; **38** Vatican Museums, AA/J Holmes; **38/39** Sistine Chapel, AA/S McBride; **40/41t** Castel Sant'Angelo, AA/S McBride; **40/41b** Castel Sant'Angelo, view over the Tiber, AA/S McBride; **42** Colosseum at night, AA/S McBride; **42/43** Colossum, AA/A Kouprianoff; **44** Atrium Vestae, Foro Romano, AA/A Kouprianoff; **44/45** Foro Romano, AA/S McBride; **46** Musei Capitolini, AA/S McBride; **46/47** Palazzo dei Conservatoi, part of Musei Capitolini, AA/S McBride; **47** Musei Capitolini, AA/S McBride; **48/49** Palazzo Barberini, AA/P Wilson; **49** Raphael's La Fornarina, Palazzo Berberini, AA/P Wilson; **50/51** Pantheon, AA/S McBride; **52t** Piazza Navona, AA/S McBride; **52c** Piazza Navona, AA/S McBride; **53** Piazza Navona, AA/A Kouprianoff; **54c** San Clemente, AA/D Miterdiri; **54b** San Clemente, AA/J Holmes; **55** San Clemente, AA/S McBride; **56/57** Pincio Gardens, AA/A Kouprianoff; **58** Scooter, Rome, AA/J Holmes; **60** San Giovanni in Laterano, AA/S McBride; **61** Santa Maria Sopra Minerva, AA/C Sawyer; **62** Vatican, AA/J Holmes; **64** Pantheon, AA/S McBride; **64/65t** Campo de' Fiori, AA/C Sawyer; **64/65b** Piazza del Popolo, AA/A Kouprianoff; **66/67** View of St Peter's Square, AA/S McBride; **69** Carving on Palazzo Spada, AA/S McBride; **70/71** Santa Maria Maggiore, AA/S McBride; **73** Terme di Caracalla, AA/D Miterdiri; **74** Basilica di Santi Giovanni e Paolo, AA/D Miterdiri; **74/75t** Arco di Constatino, AA/S McBride; **74/75b** San Paolo Fuori le Mura, AA/C Sawyer; **77** Cimitero Protestante, Keats' Grave, AA/C Sawyer; **78** Statue of Alfredo Orianai, Domus Aurea, AA/S McBride; **78/79** Foro di Cesari, in Foro Imperiali, AA/T Souter; **80/81t** Foro di Traiano, AA/J Holmes; **80/81b** Monumento Vittorio Emanuele II, AA/P Wilson; **82** Museo della Civilta Romana, AA/J Holmes; **82/83** Palatino, Domus Augustana, AA/S McBride; **84** Palazzo Colonna, AA/J Holmes; **85** Piramide di Ciao Coctio, AA/J Holmes; **86** Porte San Sebastiano, AA; **86/87** San Giovanni in Laterano, AA/S McBride; **87** Santa Croce in Gerusalemme, AA/S McBride; **88/90** Santa Maria in Cosmedin, AA/J Holmes; **90/91** Santa Sabina, AA; **92/93** San Pietro in Vincoli, AA/J Holmes; **92** Michaelangelo's Moses, San Pietro in Vincoli, AA/J Holmes; **93** Santa Sabina, AA/J Holmes; **94/95** Terme di Caracalla, AA/D Miterdiri; **94** Terme di Caracalla, AA/S McBride; **95** Mercati di Testaccio, AA/C Sawyer; **101** Giancolo, AA/S McBride; **102** Campo de' Fiori, AA/C Sawyer; **103** Chiesa Nuova, AA/D Miterdiri; **104** Colonna di Marcus Aurelius, AA/C Sawyer; **105** Fontana delle Tartarughe, AA/A Kouprianoff; **106/107** Santissimo Nome di Gesu, AA/J Holmes; **107t** Ghetto, AA/S McBride; **107b** Gianicolo, AA/D Miterdiri; **108/109** Isola Tiberina, AA/J Holmes; **110/111** Isola Tiberina, AA/A Kouprianoff; **113** Palazzo Doria, AA/P Wilson; **114** Palazzo Madama, AA; **115** Palazzo di Montecitorio, AA/J Holmes; **116/117** Palazzo Venezia, AA; **118** Piazza Farnese, AA/S McBride; **119** Ponte Sant'Angelo, AA/S McBride; **120** Sant'Agostino, AA/D Miterdiri; **120/121** Sant'Andrea della Valle, AA/J Holmes; **121** Santa Cecilia in Trastevere, AA/J Holmes; **122/123** Sant'Ivo Alla Sapienza, AA/A Kouprianoff; **124** Bernini's obelisk and elephant, AA/A Kouprianoff; **124/125** Basilica di Santa Maria in Trastevere, AA/S McBride; **126/127** Teatro di Marcello, AA/J Holmes; **127** Villa Farnesina, AA/A Kouprianoff; **135/137** Santa Maria Maggiore, AA/S McBride; **136** Ara Pacis Augustae, AA/D Miterdiri; **138/139** Fontana di Trevi, AA/S McBride; **139** Statue of Paolina Borghese, Galleria Borghese, AA/D Miterdiri; **140/141** Keats-Shelley Museum, AA/D Miterdiri; **142/143** Museo Nazionale Romano, AA/J Holmes; **144** Palazzo del Quirinale, AA/J Holmes; **144/145** Piazza Barberini, AA/S McBride; **146/147** Piazza di Spagna, AA/C Sawyer; **148** San Carlo a la Quattro Fontana, AA/C Sawyer; **149** Assumption of the Virgin, by Carracci, in Santa Maria de Popolo, AA/J Holmes; **150** Santa Pudenziana, AA/J Holmes; **151** Via Condotti, AA/S McBride; **161** Museo Gregoriano Egizio, AA/J Holmes; **162/163** Biblioteca Apostolica Vaticana, AA/P Wilson; **164** Museo Chiaramonti, AA/J Holmes; **165** Museu Gregoriano Egizio, AA/J Holmes; **166** Vatican Museums, Map Room, AA/S McBride; **166/167** Vatican Museums, Map Room, AA/S McBride; **168/169** Pinacoteca Vaticana, AA/P Wilson; **172/173** Villa Adriana, AA/S McBride; **175t/175b** Cerveteri, Etruscan barrow tombs, AA/T Souter; **176** Frascati, AA/S McBride; **177/178** Ostia Antica, AA/S McBride; **178/179** Villa d'Este, AA/S McBride; **180, 181** Tivola, Villa Adriana, AA/S McBride.

Every effort has been made to trace the copyright holders, and we apologize in advance for any accidental errors. We would be happy to apply the corrections in the following edition of this publication.

Sight locator index

Questionnaire

Dear Traveler

Your comments, opinions and recommendations are very important to us.
So please help us to improve our travel guides by taking a few minutes to
complete this simple questionnaire.

Send to: **Essential Guides,**
MailStop 64, 1000 AAA Drive, Heathrow, FL 32746–5063

Your recommendations…

We always encourage readers' recommendations for restaurants, nightlife
or shopping – if your recommendation is added to the next edition of the
guide, we will send you a FREE AAA Essential Guide of your choice.
Please state below the establishment name, location and your reasons for
recommending it.

_____

_____

_____

_____

Please send me AAA Essential _____

About this guide…

Which title did you buy?

_____ **AAA Essential**

Where did you buy it? _____

When? m m / y y

Why did you choose a AAA Essential Guide? _____

_____

_____

Did this guide meet with your expectations?

Exceeded ☐   Met all ☐   Met most ☐   Fell below ☐

Please give your reasons _____

_____

_____

_____

continued on next page…

Were there any aspects of this guide that you particularly liked? _____

_____

_____

_____

_____

Is there anything we could have done better? _____

_____

_____

_____

_____

About you...

Name (Mr/Mrs/Ms) _____

Address _____

_____

_____ **Zip** _____

Daytime tel nos. _____

Which age group are you in?

Under 25 ☐   25–34 ☐   35–44 ☐   45–54 ☐   55–64 ☐   65+ ☐

How many trips do you make a year?

Less than one ☐   One ☐   Two ☐   Three or more ☐

Are you a AAA member?   Yes ☐   No ☐

Name of AAA club _____

About your trip

When did you book? m m / y y   **When did you travel?** m m / y y

How long did you stay? _____

Was it for business or leisure? _____

Did you buy any other travel guides for your trip?   Yes ☐   No ☐

If yes, which ones? _____

_____

Thank you for taking the time to complete this questionnaire.